The Best Orchids for Indoors

Charles Marden Fitch

EDITOR

Janet Marinelli
SERIES EDITOR

Sigrun Wolff Saphire
SENIOR EDITOR

David Horak
TECHNICAL EDITOR

Kerry Barringer
SCIENCE EDITOR

Tricia Chambers
ART DIRECTOR

Joni Blackburn
COPY EDITOR

Steven Clemants
VICE-PRESIDENT,
SCIENCE &
PUBLICATIONS

Judith D. Zuk
PRESIDENT

Elizabeth Scholtz
DIRECTOR
EMERITUS

All photographs by
Charles Marden Fitch,
except as noted on
page 114.

Handbook #177

Copyright © 2004 by Brooklyn Botanic Garden, Inc.

All-Region Guides, formerly *21st-Century Gardening Series,* are published three times a year at 1000 Washington Ave., Brooklyn, NY 11225.

Subscription included in Brooklyn Botanic Garden subscriber membership dues ($35 per year; $45 outside the United States).

ISBN # 1-889538-60-4

Printed by Science Press, a division of the Mack Printing Group. Printed on recycled paper.

Above: *Cymbidium* Tiny Tiger, a hybrid with cascading inflorescences.
Cover: *Beallara* Purple Passion 'Talisman Cove'

The Best Orchids for Indoors

Orchids and How They Grow

David Horak

The orchids are generally considered to be the most diverse plant family, with estimates of their numbers ranging from 20,000 to 30,000 species in over 800 genera. This represents about 10 percent of all flowering plant species. Recent DNA research suggests that the orchids, at more than 90,000,000 years old, are among the most ancient flowering plant families. They are still evolving rapidly into new species. For example, many endemic species in the genus *Telipogon* are found in the Andes Mountains in areas that were buried under glaciers as recently as 10,000 years ago.

Like all monocots, including irises, lilies, and gingers, orchids are flowering plants that have only one seed leaf and typically lack woody tissue. However, orchids are noteworthy for having the most specialized flowers and habits in the entire group. Among the most distinctive characteristics of orchids are their flowers. All orchids have a single reproductive structure, called the column, which is formed by the fusion of the male stamens and female style (see "Orchids and Their Pollinators," page 10). These are separate in the flowers of the other families listed above. Orchids also have a modified third petal called a lip or labellum and produce enormous numbers of very tiny seeds.

Where Orchids Live

Orchids are found on all continents except Antarctica, from above the Arctic Circle in the north to Tierra del Fuego and Macquarie Island in the south. However, the vast

Orchids are found on all continents except Antarctica, but the vast majority, such as *Dendrobium delacourii,* opposite, which grows in Thailand, are native to the tropics.

The quantity and diversity of orchid species are greatest in tropical montane forests, at elevations from about 3,000 to 10,000 feet.

majority of orchid species are native to the tropics, and their numbers increase with proximity to the equator. Many orchid species are endemic, meaning they are found only in a very specific area, such as a particular mountain ridge, and nowhere else. The richest diversity of orchid species is found in the lush tropical forests of equatorial South America, Southeast Asia, and New Guinea. New species are constantly being discovered, particularly in these areas.

Orchids tend to be associated with hot, steamy tropical jungles, and many do come from these areas. In Borneo, for instance, orchids reach their greatest expression in the hot lowland forests from sea level up to about 3,000 feet in elevation. But in most of the tropics, the quantity and diversity of species increases dramatically from about 3,000 to 10,000 feet in the moderate climates of wet, montane forests. Here daytime temperatures average 70°F to 80°F, and nights are 15 to 20 degrees cooler. At higher elevations, the quantity and variety of orchids diminish, reaching their limit in the snow and cold above 14,000 feet.

Orchids vary tremendously in size. Several of the *Vanilla* species, a genus of vining orchids, can reach more than 100 feet in length, and *Sobralia altissimum,* from Peru, has been recorded at up to 44 feet in height. But for sheer mass, the king is *Grammatophyllum speciosum;* native to Southeast Asia, it perches in the crotches of large trees and produces growths up to 20 feet long and clumps weighing over two tons. The smallest orchid is probably *Platystele jungermannioides,* which is less than a quarter of an inch tall.

Growth Habits

The family is so large and widely distributed that it is no surprise that orchids exhibit a remarkable diversity of growth forms and survival strategies. Most orchids are either epiphytes or terrestrials, though they may also be lithophytic (grow on rocks) or, in the case of *Habenaria repens,* aquatic.

Epiphytes Approximately 70 percent of all orchids are epiphytes, plants that grow on other plants. Epiphytic orchids are largely confined to the tropics and subtropics, where day length and the aspect of the sun vary little with the seasons and temperature ranges are generally stable and above freezing. While almost any part of a tree can be host to epiphytic orchids, the largest number of orchid species prefer the inner branches and limbs of large, mature trees, midway up, in lightly shaded conditions. Certain tree species consistently harbor orchids. Rough-barked trees that allow some moisture to remain in the cracks and crevices tend to be more conducive to orchid growth than smooth-barked trees. However, for some epiphytes, bark quality is not important as long as there is an accumulation of humus, or organic debris.

Typically, epiphytic orchids have prominent, succulent stems called pseudobulbs that enable them to endure dry periods. Their leaves may be thin and deciduous or leathery and persistent. Their root systems are not as extensive as those of terrestrial orchids but are highly efficient at quickly absorbing moisture and nutrients. Epiphytic orchids are not parasites; they derive no nutrients directly from their hosts. However this is not to say that orchids are never detrimental to the trees. Frequently the weight of epiphytic orchids, mosses, and accumulated wet organic debris on the limbs of large trees can cause them to break off and crash to the ground.

Terrestrials As the name suggests, terrestrial orchids grow on the ground, rooting in humus. For example, it is common for orchids, such as most paphiopedilums, to be found growing in a layer of humus over the top of rocks and clay. Rather than pseudobulbs, many terrestrials such as *Nervilia* and *Anoectochilus* species have well-developed subsurface tubers, corms, or thick fleshy roots. Generally these orchids have thin leaves, often with attractive patterns. Interestingly, the two species of the genus *Rhizanthella* native to Australia not only grow in soil but grow completely underground; only their flowers rise to the soil surface to be pollinated by insects.

Obtaining Nutrients

Orchids, like plants in other families, have evolved a number of strategies for obtaining nutrients. Most orchids obtain sustenance from rotting leaves and other organic

Most epiphytic orchids, such as this *Catasetum*, come from areas with a pronounced dry period and have permanent pseudobulbs in which moisture is stored.

matter that falls or washes down around the plant. Orchids in the genus *Catasetum* develop masses of fine, rigid, vertical "basket" or "nest" roots around their bases. These roots trap and concentrate leaves and other organic debris around the plants, creating miniature compost heaps that give the plants an advantage in the competition for food.

Some orchids, called myrmecophytes, have developed symbiotic relationships with ants to obtain nutrients. *Coryanthes* species grow almost exclusively in large arboreal ant nests where their roots can readily take advantage of the accumulated organic debris. These species have seeds with oily appendages called eliaosomes that attract the ants, which then carry the seeds back to their nests. In a more complex physical adaptation, species such as *Schomburgkia tibicinis* have large, thick pseudobulbs that become hollow as they age. A small opening at the base eventually appears, allowing ants to build their nests within the pseudobulbs. The nature of this relationship is not completely understood, but the orchids probably obtain a nutritional benefit as accumulated leaf litter and dead insect carcasses decay in and around the plants. The ants also effectively protect the flowers and buds from foraging leaf-eating insects and wildlife.

Adapting to Tropical Climes

While temperate climates experience dramatic seasonal swings in temperature and day length, the tropics are usually defined by somewhat warmer or cooler periods or pronounced wet and dry periods. Some places experience little if any variation, and others go for months at a time without significant rainfall, then are deluged by a wet season of daily downpours.

Tropical orchids have adapted to the wet and dry cycles in various ways. In areas where moisture and temperature are consistent in all seasons, most orchids lack pseudobulbs, or their pseudobulbs are noticeably less developed. In shady situations the plants usually have thin, persistent leaves, such as with many species of *Paphiopedilum*. In places with higher sun exposure, the leaves tend to be stiffer and more leathery, as with *Vanda* species. These orchids are almost constantly in a state of growth, with little or no defined rest period.

The majority of epiphytic orchids, including many well-known species of *Oncidium* and *Cattleya,* come from areas with a pronounced dry period of limited duration and exposure to broken bright light. These plants tend to have prominent pseudobulbs and persistent, tough, leathery leaves.

In the harshest habitats, where the dry season is measured in months, more dramatic physical adaptations are found. Many of these plants have a specialized metabolic process typically seen in cacti, known as Crassulacean acid metabolism, or CAM, which minimizes their need for water. Typically these orchids also exhibit one of two foliage forms. In the most common adaptation, orchids, such as *Catasetum* species, have thin, deciduous leaves but prominent fleshy pseudobulbs that retain the moisture and nutrients needed to survive. Orchids such as *Brassavola nodosa* have small pseudobulbs but thick succulent leaves that function like pseudobulbs. In order to survive, the plants store moisture in the pseudobulbs or the succulent leaves.

Orchids are adapted not only to seasonal cycles but also to the effects of convectional weather. The daily cycle of warming and cooling generally results in a difference of about 15 to 20 degrees Fahrenheit between day and night temperatures; it also creates fog, dew, and, in the mountains, cloud effects.

This daily cycle also generates constant breezes that quickly dry plants up in the trees. Epiphytic orchid roots are specially adapted to these conditions. Composed of a wiry central core surrounded by thick spongy tissue called velamen, they are able to clasp tree bark and quickly soak up moisture before it can run off or evaporate.

Paphiopedilum callosum, which grows on jungle slopes in Malaysia, has a terrestrial growth habit.

Orchids and Their Pollinators

David Horak

Some flowering plants are promiscuous, relying on enticement and reward to lure whatever insect comes along. But orchids typically have exclusive relationships with their pollinators. These are usually bees, wasps, and flies, but many orchids also utilize moths, butterflies, fungus gnats, or birds to cross-pollinate their flowers. While the ways that various species entice pollinators to visit their flowers and carry their pollinia (pollen masses) off to a flower on another plant vary tremendously, they often employ complex, frequently deceptive strategies to achieve success.

Bloom Time

Governed by the weather and pollinator activity, orchids regulate their bloom time to increase the likelihood of successful pollination. The length of time that flowers remain open and viable varies considerably from a few hours in *Flickingeria* species to as much as nine months in species such as *Dendrobium cuthbertsonii*.

Some orchids flower only once or twice a year at very specific times. Others have flowers opening so frequently during the course of the year that they are almost constantly in bloom. Orchids that bloom frequently or for extended periods certainly have less difficulty coordinating blooming with others of their kind, increasing the chances of successful cross-pollination. By contrast, species with short bloom periods

Many orchids employ complex and often deceptive strategies to entice pollinators to visit their flowers and carry their pollinia (pollen masses) to another flower. In *Catasetum* flowers, opposite, pollinia are ejected when the pollinator touches a specifically placed trigger—they are literally shot onto the insect's back.

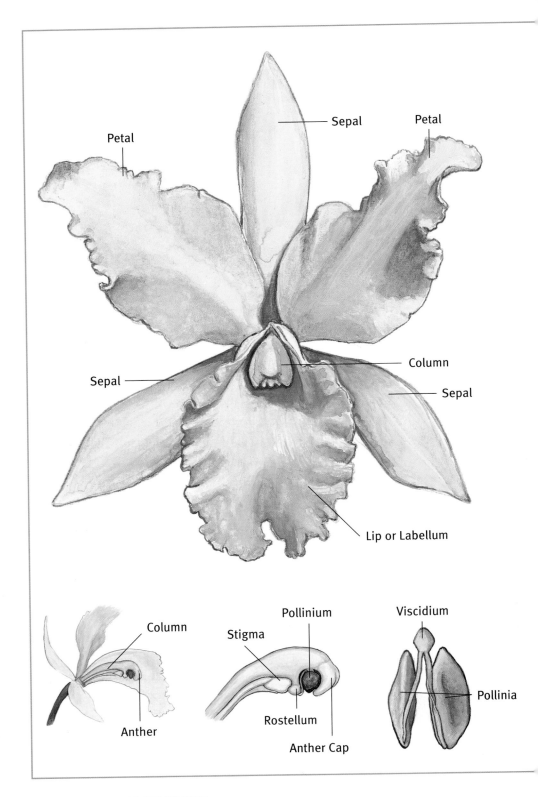

Petal

Sepal

Petal

Petal

Sepal

Column

Sepal

Lip or Labellum

Column

Anther

Stigma

Pollinium

Rostellum

Anther Cap

Viscidium

Pollinia

Anatomy of an Orchid Flower

Despite the astonishing diversity found in the thousands of wild species and man-made hybrids, orchid flowers show an unmistakable family resemblance. Orchid flowers are generally bilaterally symmetrical—only a single imaginary line can be drawn through a flower to create a mirror image.

A typical orchid flower has three sepals (the outer segments that protect the bud before the flower opens), alternating with three petals. The petals and sepals may be similar or not, showy or inconspicuous.

The middle petal, which is always opposite the column, is usually quite different from the others. Called the lip or labellum, it comes in a variety of shapes, depending on the species, and can be wavy or fringed or covered with hairs or other structures. The labellum often serves as a landing pad and attractant for insect pollinators.

The most distinctive aspect of orchid floral anatomy is the column, the single reproductive structure formed by the fusion of the male stamens and female style, which are separated in the vast majority of plant families. Most orchids have a single fertile anther (flower structure where pollen is produced) located at the tip of the column.

In most orchids, pollen is not loose and granular when ripe but rather is packed into a waxy mass called a pollinium. Pollinia usually occur in pairs, but in some species they are found in groups of up to eight. The pollinia typically share a single small sticky tab called a viscidium, which adheres to the pollinator when contact is made.

To discourage self-pollination and promote cross-pollination, the pollinia typically are separated from the stigma (female part of the flower that receives the pollen) by a flap of tissue called the rostellum. The rostellum also aids in the transfer of the pollinia from the pollinator to the stigma.

There are exceptions to the typical orchid flower configuration, shown opposite. For example, slipper orchids such as paphiopedilums, considered a primitive branch of the orchid family, have a pouch- or slipper-shaped labellum, below left. They also have two fertile anthers instead of a single anther, below right. A third anther has evolved into a fleshy plate, called a staminode, which sits in front of the other two and assists in luring and guiding pollinators across the anthers and stigma.

 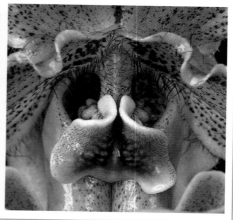

Microtis parviflora, left, lures its ant pollinator with a reward of nectar. *Prasophyllum fimbria,* right, uses deception to attract its pollinators: It seems to offer a food reward but doesn't.

would seem to be at a severe disadvantage. Orchids in the New World genus *Sobralia,* whose flowers typically are open for no more than one day, solve this problem by relying on a group temperature signal to achieve simultaneous bloom. Several days after a trigger temperature is reached, all the individual plants in a given population flower at the same time.

Lures and Rewards

Orchids utilize a variety of intricate strategies for attracting the many specific pollinators on which their survival depends. In virtually all cases the orchid and pollinator have evolved together.

Orchids commonly use nectar to entice their pollinators, but they also employ color, shape, or fragrance, and even mimic the flowers of other plants. Color is often important for animals active during the day. For example, orchids pollinated by hummingbirds and butterflies tend to have red, orange, or pink tubular—but not necessarily fragrant—flowers. They frequently have yellow blotchy patterns to mimic the anthers and pollen of the other plant types visited by these nectar lovers, but this mimicry is deceptive because the orchids often offer no nectar reward. The flowers of most moth-pollinated species, such as angraecoids, are green or white and are often very fragrant only at night so they can be found by these primarily night-flying

Some orchids lure their pollinators through sexual deception. *Oncidium henekenii,* above, is pollinated by male bees trying to mate with the flower, which resembles a female bee.

insects. The flowers of orchids pollinated by flies or carrion beetles, such as many of the *Bulbophyllum* species, typically come in browns and fleshy reds and emit the odor of rotting meat. The stench of *Bulbophyllum beccarii* is so foul that it has been said to smell like "a herd of dead elephants."

Little iridescent euglossine bees can be seen buzzing in the canopies of Central American forests when the bucket orchids (*Coryanthes*) are in bloom. As the name suggests, in these species the lip of the flower forms a bucket filled with a sweet-scented viscous liquid. Just above, they also have a rounded pad from which the male bees scrape off fragrant oils they pack into sacks on their back legs and use to court females. Actually elaborate traps, the surface of the flower is slippery, and occasionally a bee loses his footing and falls into the bucket. The only way to escape and avoid drowning is through a narrow opening at the base of the lip. As the bee squeezes his way through, his back scrapes against the column and the two pollinia are deposited on his back. Fortunately for the orchids, the bees seem to have short memories and are easily fooled: After drying himself and flying off, the bee will often visit another flower and repeat the process, this time depositing the pollinia on the stigma (female part) of the flower.

Some orchid flowers deceive their pollinators by mimicking the appearance and scents produced by female insects. In European species of the genus *Ophrys,* flowers

More sexual deception: Flowers of the beard orchid, *Calochilus robertsonii,* left, attract male scolliid wasps. At right, a male wasp pollinates *Chiloglottis reflexa* while attempting to copulate with the flower.

have a labellum that looks like the body of a fetching female bee or wasp—complete with the requisite shape, iridescent colors or colorful markings, and hairs. They also exude a scent that simulates the pheromones produced by receptive females. Each species of *Ophrys* is generally pollinated by its own species of insect. When the male lands on the flower, it grabs the labellum and attempts to copulate with it. In the process, the flower deposits pollinia on the insect's head, to be carried and placed on the next flower he visits. Other orchids, such as species of *Oncidium,* produce flowers that resemble the males of certain territorial bees or wasps. Seen as competitors, these flowers are attacked. They are shaped in such a way that the attacking insect is inevitably placed in contact with the pollinia or stigma.

Secure Attachments

Where the pollinia become physically attached to the pollinator and how they get there is individual to each given orchid species. One example involves euglossine bees, common shared pollinators for orchids in Central and South America. The structural differences in the various flowers ensure that the pollinia are attached to a part of the bee specific to each orchid species: The pollinia of one may be attached to the insect's eye, that of another to the top of the thorax, and that of still another to a foreleg. When the pollinia-loaded bee encounters an orchid flower, only the pollinia in the proper position for that species will come in contact with the stigma and accomplish pollination.

In the genus *Catasetum,* the pollinia are ejected when the pollinator touches a specifically placed trigger and are literally shot onto the insect's back. Some species of *Bulbophyllum* and *Porroglossum* have hinged lips that snap shut or tip closed, temporarily pinning the insect against the column so that the pollinia can be properly secured.

Orchid Seeds

In the wild, the chance of successful pollination varies tremendously among orchid species. In some, nearly every fertile flower is pollinated; in others, few or none are. Once pollinated, the flower begins to collapse and the ovary, located directly behind the sepals, begins to swell. The time it takes for orchid seed to mature varies from a few days to nearly a year. When finally mature, the fruit, a capsule, splits open and the seed spills out.

Most orchid species have very specific needs regarding where they are able to germinate and grow. To ensure that seeds find these ideal conditions, orchids produce vast amounts of minute seeds, which are disbursed widely by the wind. Harvard University's Oakes Ames, a prominent early-20th-century orchid researcher, report-

Pollinia have been securely attached to this male ichneumonid wasp on a *Cryptostylis ovata* flower.

Orchids produce enormous amounts of minute seeds that are disbursed widely by the wind.

edly spent a rainy afternoon counting the seeds in an individual orchid capsule and arrived at the astonishing total of 3.5 million.

Because orchid seeds are so small, however, they contain virtually no endosperm, the food reserve on which young plantlets typically depend prior to the development of roots and leaves. To germinate in the wild, tiny orchid seeds must become infected by a mycorrhizal fungus that produces substances necessary for germination and growth.

Of the very few orchid seeds that are able to find ideal conditions to germinate, few survive to maturity. It generally takes most wild orchids five to seven years to reach blooming size. Mortality rates are high during the fragile early stages of orchid growth.

Early efforts to artificially raise orchids from seed in the 19th century were unsuccessful until growers discovered that seed sowed at the base of the mother plant would sometimes germinate. This was possible because the parents were still naturally infected with the necessary mycorrhizal fungi. However, even this technique resulted in relatively few plants, so the commercial orchid industry continued to depend on vast quantities of wild-collected plants to satisfy the constant demand of wealthy collectors (see "Gardener's Guide to Orchid Conservation," page 26).

In 1922, Louis Knudson discovered that nearly 100 percent germination could be achieved by starting seeds in flasks on sterile media fortified with nutrients to feed the young plants. Some years later the process of mericloning was developed, allowing the mass production and marketing of individual cultivars. Thanks to these achievements, combined with humanity's insatiable desire to create artificial hybrids—presently more than 100,000 have been registered—today orchids are produced by the millions. They are now among the most widely grown and popular flowering pot plants in the world.

For a comprehensive discussion of orchid ecology, consult the monumental work *The Orchids: Natural History and Classification* (1981, 1990), by Robert L. Dressler. (See "For More Information," page 110.)

Because orchid seeds are so small, they have virtually no endosperm or food reserve and in the wild depend on mycorrhizal fungi to produce substances necessary for germination and growth. Many species need to be propagated in vitro on a sterile medium fortified with nutrients to feed the young plants, such as these orchids grown from seed in Bangkok.

The Classification and Naming of Orchids

Phillip Cribb

A good estimate of the number of orchid species around the world is 25,000, but there may well be 30,000, given the rate at which orchids are still being discovered. This is far too many species for any one person to remember. Classification helps make these vast numbers more manageable.

The earliest attempts at orchid classification grouped "like with like," relying almost entirely upon the characteristics of the flower. The more ambitious classifications of recent years have tried to group together orchids that are related in an evolutionary sense.

Early Classification Systems

During the late 18th and early 19th centuries, exotic orchids flowed into Europe, particularly the British Isles, from the tropics of India, Southeast Asia, and the Americas, and the mania for growing orchids began. Ideally placed in London, where he was assistant secretary to the Horticultural Society of London and professor of Botany at King's College, John Lindley (1799–1865) became the

Many orchid species, such as *Oncidium cucullatum,* above, display a fantastic array of colors, shapes, and patterns. In the search for more unusual flowers, orchid breeders discovered that it is possible to cross orchid species not only with others in the same genus but also with members of other genera to create complex hybrids, such as *Colmanara* Wildcat, opposite.

acknowledged expert on orchids. In his *Genera and Species of Orchidaceous Plants* (1830–40), Lindley produced the first significant scientific classification of the family. He distinguished seven major groups within the orchid family based on features of the column, which bears both the male (anthers) and female (stigmas) organs. In particular he considered the number of anthers and the manner in which they hold pollen.

The first major departure from orchid classifications relying almost exclusively on characteristics of the flower was proposed by Ernst Pfitzer (1846–1906). His scheme incorporated vegetative as well as floral characteristics. Rudolf Schlechter's classification scheme, published posthumously in *Notizblatt des Botanischen Gartens Berlin, Dahlem* in 1926, incorporated many of Pfitzer's ideas as well as those of Lindley and other early orchid specialists. Like its predecessors, it places like with like on the basis of both floral and vegetative features. The result is a useful scheme in which the major divisions within the family are firmly outlined, and it has been widely followed since it was published.

Not surprisingly, the ideas on the evolution of living organisms outlined by Charles Darwin in *On the Origin of Species* (1860) have had a great influence on the thinking of botanists. At first this led to classification systems that suggested that overall similarity reflected evolutionary relationships. However, convergent or parallel evolution (evolution of similar traits in plants that are not closely related) is widespread in the orchids, and quite unrelated species can look alike. Therefore, more recently fresh attempts have been made to produce classifications that better reflect orchid evolution.

Modern Orchid Classification

The most widely used classification system of recent years is that of Robert Dressler in *The Orchids: Natural History and Classification* (1981, 1990). Dressler used evidence from floral and vegetative characteristics, anatomy, cytology, and breeding behavior to construct a scheme that recognizes six subfamilies. The Apostasioideae, with two or three anthers, are a primitive group comprising two genera seldom seen in cultivation. The Cypripedioideae, the well-known slipper orchids, are also rather primitive, with two anthers and a characteristic slipper-shaped lip. The remaining four subfamilies—the Spiranthoideae, Orchidoideae, Epidendroideae, and Vandoideae—all have flowers with a single anther. The vast majority of cultivated orchids belong to the last two subfamilies. The Epidendroideae includes genera such as *Cattleya, Laelia, Sophronitis, Coelogyne, Vanilla,* and, of course, *Epidendrum* itself. The

DNA analysis suggests that vandas don't form their own subfamily of orchids. Above: *Vanda sanderiana*. Below: *Vanda lamellata* var. *boxallii*.

Vandoideae contains genera such as *Cymbidium, Oncidium, Odontoglossum, Miltonia, Vanda,* and *Phalaenopsis.* Dressler suggested that his 1981 system reflects not only similarity but also the evolutionary advance of the orchids from the primitive Apostasioideae to the highly evolved Epidendroideae and Vandoideae. There are, however, species in each subfamily with primitive features, suggesting that orchid evolution has not been straightforward.

Pamela Burns-Balogh and Vicky Funk were the first to apply cladistics to a data set of orchid morphological features, in 1986. Cladistics is a method of reconstructing the evolutionary history of living organisms by determining which features are ancestral ("primitive") and which are derived (more "advanced"). Computers have provid-

ed the technology essential in analyzing the large data sets necessary to produce the resulting "family trees," called cladograms. In 1993, Dressler published an update of his classification incorporating cladistic analysis. Nowadays, cladistics is commonplace in orchid classification, especially since DNA analysis has become a standard technique, providing thousands of new characters for assessing evolutionary relationships. A detailed new classification of the orchid family incorporating DNA analysis is being published in six volumes by Oxford Univerity Press under the title *Genera Orchidacearum*.

DNA analysis has confirmed many aspects of the established orchid classifications but has also provided some surprises. It has upheld the view that the orchid family is monophyletic—that all members of the family derive from the same ancestral species. It has also confirmed Dressler's conclusion that the subfamilies Apostasioideae, Cypripedioideae, and Orchidoideae are all monophyletic. However, recent work clearly shows that *Vanilla* and its relatives form a separate and ancient lineage and deserve recognition as the subfamily Vanilloideae; that the Spiranthoideae nest within a more broadly defined Orchidoideae; and that Vandoideae are a specialized lineage within a more broadly defined Epidendroideae. Thus, the most recent classification suggests that the orchids comprise five subfamilies: Apostasioideae, Cypripedioideae, Vanilloideae, Orchidoideae, and Epidendroideae. This methodology is also beginning to influence the classification of tribes and subtribes.

It also suggests that our present concepts of orchid genera need to be considerably revised. A paper published in *Lindleyana* in 2000 on the *Cattleya* alliance has proposed significant changes to the circumscription of genera as well known as *Laelia* and *Sophronitis*. While this paper, as well as others proposing reclassification of subtribes as diverse as Orchidinae and Oncidiinae, is ruffling feathers—no one likes name changes—breeders often find that the new thinking is in line with the breeding behavior they observe among various orchid groups. Changing ideas on the classification of orchids has had and likely will continue to have profound effects upon the naming of orchids and upon the registration of orchid hybrids in the future.

How Classification Helps Orchid Growers

All growers want their orchids to be identified and named correctly. It is in this way that classification can be a great help. If growers recognize in an unnamed plant features common to other plants in their collection, they will be able to place the plant in its correct genus, or at least close by. Then, by referring to one of the many excellent orchid identification manuals, it is usually possible to make an accurate identification fairly rapidly.

Understanding how orchids are classified can help growers not only to know their plants better but also to grow them better. Close proximity in a classification system

Units of Orchid Classification

In all classifications of living organisms, the basic unit is the species. Several other categories at higher ranks are also used in orchid classification. Beginning with Orchidaceae, the orchid family, at the top, they are the following:

Subfamily: In the most recent system, five subfamilies are recognized (see page 24). The names of subfamilies end in -oideae.

Tribe: Subfamilies are divided into tribes, whose names end in -eae.

Subtribe: Awareness of the subtribe is particularly useful in orchid breeding, because species and genera within a subtribe are often interfertile and constitute a breeding group—for example,

Anguloa clowesii.

Oncidiinae, Laeliinae, and Pleurothallidinae. The names of subtribes end in -inae.

Genus: Species that are closely allied and morphologically similar are placed in the same genus. Some degree of crossability, which in orchids may be considerable, is also possible among species in a genus. Species that are relatively distinct and not closely related are placed in different genera. Genus names end in a variety of letters, often in *-us* (masculine), *-a* (feminine), and *-um* (neuter).

Species: In most cases, orchid species are delineated on the basis of morphology alone (that is, according to the structure of their flowers and vegetative parts).

The following shows how a particular orchid, *Anguloa clowesii,* fits within the entire orchid family, as reclassified in *Genera Orchidacearum* using DNA analysis:

Family: Orchidaceae

Subfamily: Epidendroideae

Tribe: Epidendreae

Subtribe: Maxillariinae

Genus: *Anguloa*

Species: *Anguloa clowesii*

Other terms are used to describe groups of orchids for horticultural purposes. The term "alliance" is used to designate a group of genera that have many common characteristics and can be used for breeding to produce new hybrid genera. An alliance is limited to genera within a single tribe. The term "grex" refers to a group of cultivars with the same parentage (see page 27).

may provide clues to the cultural requirements of unfamiliar species. For example, growers can better predict a new species' sensitivity to various pest controls if they know the sensitivity of closely related species.

Because modern classification systems such as that of *Genera Orchidacearum* attempt to place together orchids that are related to each other in terms of both overall similarity and evolution, breeders can consult them for fresh possibilities for their crossing programs. The breeding compatibility of species in such genera as *Cattleya, Laelia, Sophronitis, Schomburgkia,* and *Epidendrum* is well known. Not surprisingly, these genera are closely allied in recent classification. In *The Orchids: Natural History and Classification* (1981, 1990), Dressler lists 57 genera as closely allied to *Oncidium* and 86 genera close to *Phalaenopsis*—surely here lie the building blocks for future hybridizing programs.

I believe that the new classification systems will be more useful than the present widely used schemes based mainly upon morphological characteristics, but it will take time for them to infiltrate horticulture. I am reminded that the name *Paphiopedilum* for the tropical Asiatic slipper orchids took 72 years from the time it was proposed by Ernst Pfitzer until it was adopted by the International Orchid Registration Authority. No one likes to change names that have been used for many years, but modern classification techniques will undoubtedly provide fresh insights into the orchids, the most diverse and fascinating family of flowering plants.

Orchid Names

Anyone interested in orchids, whether orchid grower or scientist, can communicate about a particular plant if it is correctly identified and named. The scientific names for orchids have acquired widespread use because few have common names.

Species Scientific names are subject to the rules of nomenclature laid out in the *International Code of Botanical Nomenclature* (2000). The names of species usually consist of two parts, the genus name followed by the specific epithet, which identifies one particular species in the genus. These may be followed by one or more personal names, often abbreviated, called the authority or authorities, which represent the name of the botanist who first described the species as new to science and, if applicable, the botanist who reclassified the species. For example:

Genus name	Species epithet	Authority name (John Lindley)
Oncidium	*cavendishianum*	Lindl

Hybrids The names of hybrids, naturally occurring or man-made, are controlled by two codes—the *International Code of Botanical Nomenclature* and the *International Code of*

Nomenclature for Cultivated Plants (1995). Names of hybrids of two species in the same genus consist of the scientific names of the parents combined by a multiplication sign—for example, *Cattleya forbesii* × *C. loddigesii.* Natural hybrids can be given their own specific epithet: *Paphiopedilum* × *siamense* is the natural cross of *P. callosum* × *P. appletonianum.* When two genera are involved in a cross, a hybrid genus name is formed by combining the genus names of the two parents: *Cattleya* crossed with *Laelia* gives × *Laeliocattleya.* Trigeneric hybrids and those formed from more than three genera are given a name that combines a personal surname with the ending -ara. Thus, *Rolfeara* is *Sophronitis* × *Cattleya* ×

Masdevallia **Marguerite. Masdevallias are part of the Pleurothallid Alliance, a group of genera that have many common characteristics and can be cross-bred.**

Brassavola. The multiplication sign is often left out when writing about hybrid genera.

Groups of orchid cultivars with the same parentage are given grex names. The registration of grex names is undertaken by the International Orchid Registration Authority, currently the Royal Horticultural Society in London. Cultivar names are also used for orchids, but usually only if a particular clone of a grex has been awarded; abbreviations of the award and the organization that granted it often follow the cultivar name. The name of *Vuylsteakeara* Cambria 'Plush', one of the most widely grown orchids in the world, with crimson sepals and petals, a white lip dotted with crimson, and a yellow crest, has the following components:

Genus name	Grex name	Cultivar name
Vuylsteakeara	Cambria	'Plush'

(*Vuylsteakeara* is a tri-generic cross of *Miltonia, Odontoglossum,* and *Cochlioda.*)

A detailed account of the naming and registration of orchids is given in *The Handbook on Orchid Nomenclature and Registration* (1993).

Gardener's Guide to Orchid Conservation

We've come a long way from the days of gung-ho orchid collecting. In the 19th century, efforts to artificially raise orchids from seed were frequently unsuccessful, so the commercial orchid industry continued to depend on vast quantities of wild-collected plants to feed the insatiable demands of wealthy collectors. Often hundreds of thousands of plants taken from jungles around the world would perish during the long sea voyage to Europe. Wild-collected orchids were seen as an inexhaustible resource of vast tropical forests around the world. We now realize that this is not the case.

A few orchids, such as paphiopedilums and phragmipediums, are still threatened by collectors who dig them up in the wild. However, new laws to help protect them from harmful exploitation have been put in place, such as the Convention on International Trade in Endangered Species of Wild Flora and Fauna (CITES— see page 29). These laws have encouraged efforts to raise orchid species from seed and via tissue culture using

Tropical forest in El Salvador going up in smoke. Habitat loss is by far the greatest threat to orchids worldwide.

advanced in vitro techniques. Today, by far the greatest threat to orchids worldwide is habitat loss. Countless acres of tropical forest, the centers of orchid diversity, are lost each year due to farming and timber extraction.

The protection of orchid habitats, combined with artificial propagation of selected species, will not only help save rare orchids but also bring economic benefits to tropical nations. A well-planned program between the government and private businesses can earn money through local orchid sales, tourism, and controlled exports of artificially propagated plants. Sometimes orchid culture is combined with other social programs. A good example is Thailand's Royal Project, in which army specialists work with Thai horticulturists to teach hill-tribe peoples how to grow orchids as an alternative to cultivating opium for export. Orchids are a good substitute for expensive illegal crops because they have a high resale value and grow well in the region.

Orchid growers in temperate regions can also play an important role in orchid conservation. Following are some suggestions.

- The vast majority of orchids available for purchase in North America are hybrids created by orchid breeders. Purchasing man-made hybrids poses little or no threat to rare orchid species in their native habitats.

- Do not purchase orchid species that have been collected from the wild. Ask suppliers about the origin of their plants and ask to see import permits. Buy orchids that have been certifiably propagated by seed or tissue culture. Purchasing flasked seedlings is a guarantee that the plants have been artificially propagated.

- Become aware of which species are most threatened by international trade and how CITES aims to protect them (see www.cites.org).

- Join an orchid society and support or help establish an active conservation committee. The American Orchid Society has been involved in orchid conservation programs for many years (see page 111).

- If you grow orchid species, help conserve their genetic diversity by propagating them by seed, producing seed capsules via cross-pollination. Share plants and pollen with other conservation-minded orchid growers. Keep accurate records of the provenance of the plants and pollen.

- Read the World Conservation Union (IUCN) Species Survival Commission's action plan for orchids. Among the specific actions recommended are identification and protection of areas rich in orchid species, and encouraging the propagation of rare and new species for commercial development to reduce demand for plants collected from the wild. The plan's executive summary and information on ordering are available online at www.iucn.org/themes/ssc/pubs/orchids.htm.

The Best Way to Obtain Orchids

Charles Marden Fitch

To increase your chance of success with orchids, choose plants that do best in the environment you can provide. For example, if you have sunny windows in a warm home, ascocendas, epidendrums, and many *Cattleya* hybrids should do well. For less intense light choose *Phalaenopsis, Paphiopedilum,* and *Brassia* selections. Growing orchids under artificial lights gives you control over light intensity, so temperature range will be the major consideration in choosing suitable orchids.

Visit a commercial orchid grower, local orchid society sales table, or major orchid show. In these places you can study orchids in bloom and ask the experts questions. Another useful hunting venue is a botanical garden that displays orchids; many have gift shops that sell orchids.

When you are ready to buy, look for orchid hybrids or artificially propagated species (see "Gardener's Guide to Orchid Conservation," page 28). At a major commercial orchid nursery, you can select from many genera in bloom. Perusing orchid catalogs is another fun way to find suitable plants. Many growers also have web sites with photos, descriptions, and prices.

If you are just learning how to grow orchids, increase your chances of success by starting with mature, ready-to-bloom plants established in pots. Later, after you have refined your orchid growing practices, you can save money by buying smaller plants. Seedlings and meristem (tissue-cultured) orchids may take several years to bloom, but you can usually get several smaller plants for the price of a single flowering-size specimen.

Encyclopedia of Orchids

The encyclopedia that follows is organized by orchid genus or by alliance (group of genera that share many common characteristics and can be interbred). An introduction to each genus or alliance, written by a top expert on the group, is followed by detailed growing tips.

Note on Abbreviations of Names

When searching for a particular orchid, be aware that you will often encounter abbreviations of the genus names, both natural and man-made hybrids. For example, oncidiums (*Oncidium*) are often abbreviated as Onc. Long, multigenus hybrid names are also frequently shortened; for example, *Sophrolaeliocattleya* (a trigeneric hybrid between *Sophronitis, Laelia,* and *Cattleya*) will often appear as Slc.

Angraecoids

Charles Marden Fitch

Angraecoid orchids, most famous for the genus *Angraecum*, come from diverse habitats in Madagascar and other nearby tropical islands. Some genera are also found in East Africa. The various species and hybrids of *Angraecum* are excellent choices for mixed orchid collections because they grow well in intermediate temperatures. In my greenhouse, tall *Angraecum* hybrids grow on the southeast side where they get strong morning light. Directly above hang *Dendrobium* hybrids and some *Encyclia* hybrids that tolerate even brighter sun. Alongside the angraecums sit *Phalaenopsis* and assorted hybrids of *Oncidium*, *Miltonia*, and *Brassia*. Hailing from various parts of the tropical world these orchid genera all thrive in the same greenhouse, provided they are placed according to their light preferences.

The huge long-spurred flowers of *Angraecum sesquipedale,* a species from Madagascar, captivated the interest of naturalist Charles Darwin. Wondering how the orchid's intricate flowers were pollinated, Darwin developed the theory that some night-flying insect had to have a tongue long enough to reach the sweet nectar inside *Angraecum sesquipedale*'s 12-inch flower "tail," or spur. The flower's sweet nighttime perfume, he surmised, had to attract the insect. He predicted that the pollinator was a big moth. At the time of Darwin's informed guess, in an 1862 publication, no such insect had been documented, but 50 years later a nocturnal *Angraecum sesquipedale*–pollinating moth was discovered.

Even for humans, the long floral "tail" and waxy substance (thickness and durability) of *Angraecum* flowers combine with a pleasantly intoxicating nocturnal perfume for a dramatic effect. Species and hybrids that reach a mature size of one to

Opposite: A primary hybrid made from two large species that have proven adaptable in cultivation, *Angraecum* Ol Tukai is a popular orchid with an intoxicating nocturnal perfume.

three feet have the largest flowers; these usually form from late fall into winter, often around Christmas. The largest species include Darwin's *Angraecum sesquipedale, A. superbum,* and *A. eburneum.* These species are so adaptable in cultivation that many clones have been granted awards for cultural merit by the American Orchid Society. You will find them and their hybrids such as *Angraecum* Ol Tukai (*A. comorense* × *A. sesquipedale*), *A.* Orchidglade (*A. sesquipedale* × *A. giryamae*), and *A.* Veitchii (*A. eburneum* × *A. sesquipedale*) in several orchid catalogs. In my collection these three showy large-flowered primary hybrids grow 28 to 40 inches tall and about 24 inches across, doing well in 10- to 12-inch pots. Because the parent species are from lowland habitats, the hybrids do best with intermediate to warm nights. In my mixed collection they thrive with winter nighttime temperatures of 60°F to 65°F. Large angraecums are attractive even when not in bloom. With their broad thick leaves 15 to 17 inches long and $2^1/2$ inches wide, they look somewhat like dracaenas.

A more compact plant that also thrives with intermediate temperatures is *Angraecum leonis.* The form often seen in catalogs is from the Comoro Islands north of Madagascar. *Angraecum leonis* has night-fragrant three-inch white flowers in the winter. The compact plant has thick eight- to ten-inch-long leaves and flowers when it is six to eight inches tall.

Another compact species is *Angraecum magdalenae,* recently crossed with larger types to create some excellent hybrids including *A.* Compactolena (*A. compactum* × *A. magdalenae*), *A.* Lemforde White Beauty (*A. magdalenae* × *A. sesquipedale*), *A.* Vigulena (*A. magdalenae* × *A. viguieri*) and *A.* Superlena (*A. superbum* × *A. magdalenae*). In my collection *Angraecum* Vigulena has grown to 32 inches tall in 12 years, thriving in a six-inch clay pot with a pad of osmunda fiber around the base to encourage more roots. The fragrant four-inch white flowers usually appear in late summer and last about two weeks in perfection. My 13-year-old *Angraecum* Compactolena grows in a six-inch pot, with one eight-inch-tall offset at the base of a foot-tall main growth. Leaf spread is 15 inches across. The waxy white night-fragrant flowers appear in early fall.

Growing at elevations from 5,000 to 6,000 feet in its native habitat, the Madagascan species *Angraecum magdalenae* thrives in cooler conditions in a greenhouse; it tolerates nighttime temperatures to around 50°F. When *Angraecum magdalenae* is used as a parent with one of the larger species that prefer warmer temperatures, the offspring hybrids grow well with nighttime temperatures ranging from 55°F to 68°F. In general, hybrids are more adaptable to varied growing conditions than pure species. The hybrid

Species in the genus *Aeranthes* are crossed with *Angraecum* species to make the new genus *Angranthes*. Above is *Angranthes* Grandalena (*Angraecum magdalena* × *Aeranthes grandiflora*).

Angraecum White Emblem 'Joyce Sarah' AM/AOS (*A. didieri* × *A. magdalenae*) received an American Orchid Society Award of Merit for flower quality. Its pure white flowers are a nice blend of both species parents' flowers.

Small-Growing Angraecums

Small-growing types such as *Aerangis* and *Aeranthes* are compact enough to grow indoors under lights. The genus *Aerangis* is best known for *Aerangis luteo-alba* var. *rhodostica,* a compact selection with white flowers marked red. *Aerangis* plants do well mounted on slabs of cork bark with some coarse New Zealand sphagnum moss tucked in around the roots. To attach plants to cork bark, tree fern slabs, or even to the trunks of living tropical trees, you may try using a strip of panty hose. Available in colors that closely match the support medium and easy to stretch yet tough, a strip of panty hose will last long enough to allow an orchid to become well established with new roots gripping the underlying support.

Several *Aerangis* species come from warm East African habitats such as Uganda, where they often thrive on unpruned coffee plants. An *Aerangis collum-cygni* (*A. compta*) I attached to a coffee plant in my greenhouse established itself well and began to bloom after three years, producing pendant sprays of white flowers blushed apricot in winter. Any of the *Aerangis* species can be mounted on the trunks of coffee (*Coffea* species) or tea (*Camellia sinensis*) plants in a greenhouse or in a humid sunroom. Some of the recently created primary hybrids are easier to grow than pure species. For example, I grew *Aerangis compacta* × *A. biloba* under fluorescent lights in the basement, where it did well next to begonias, *Phalaenopsis,* and *Cattleya* seedlings with nighttime temperatures of 65°F to 68°F all year long. This primary hybrid grew to eight inches tall on a chunk of cork bark with some coarse New Zealand sphagnum moss at the base.

Aeranthes is a genus of compact white-flowered species that has been crossed with *Angraecum* to create the new genus *Angranthes*. One adaptable choice that thrives under wide-spectrum fluorescent lamps is *Angranthes* Grandalena (*Angraecum magdalenae* × *Aeranthes grandiflora*). This hybrid has been granted several American Orchid Society awards for flower quality. My mature plant of this compact *Angranthes* thrives in a four-inch pot that holds three growths, two of which are offsets produced by the main six-inch-tall, 24-year-old original plant. The low, bushy plants have leaf spans of 14 inches. The three- to four-inch white night-fragrant flowers appear in November. From late May until early September I put the plant outside under tall oaks, where it makes sturdy new leaves.

Opposite: Angraecoids such as *Angraecum* Orchidglade have thick foliage but no water-storing pseudobulbs. To keep the plants healthy, it's important to keep their roots evenly moist but not soggy.

Light The light requirements for Angraecoids are similar to those of *Phalaenopsis*. They grow well with bright diffuse light but no direct sun. The leathery-leafed *Angraecum* hybrids, such as *Angraecum* Orchidglade, *A.* Ol Tukai, and *A.* Veitchii tolerate direct morning and late-afternoon sunlight but need some midday shade to prevent sunburn.

As with other orchid genera the goal is to grow plants that produce sturdy stems with medium-green leaves. A foot-candle meter reading of 2,000 to 3,000 is the right intensity for healthy Angraecoids.

Temperatures Angraecoids come from habitats that range in altitude from sea level to over 5,000 feet on cool mountain slopes. The popular cultivated species and hybrids made from them thrive with nighttime temperatures of 60°F to 65°F Daytime temperatures should be 8 to 10 degrees higher, and up to 15 degrees higher during the prime growing season from April into October. Where air circulation is poor, provide a small fan to keep the air moving. When possible put plants outdoors during the warm summer months, returning them inside before night temperatures drop below 50°F.

Water Angraecoids have thick foliage but no water-storing pseudobulbs. Keep roots evenly moist but never soggy. When plants are growing new leaves they need more water. But be sure to watch the weather: If it's cool and not very bright, it's best to wait a few days between waterings to avoid rotting the roots. Indoors be careful that no water remains in the growing point at night. Angraecoids are monopodial orchids (they have a single stem and growing point at the tip, or crown, of the plant) with a V-shaped

growing point that holds water. With limited air circulation indoors, rot can easily start when water sits in the growing point overnight. Do overhead watering on sunny mornings to be sure surface water evaporates by night-time.

Humidity A relative humidity above 50 percent is required to grow healthy angraecoids. In warm weather, mist or sprinkle the plants in early morning. Indoors under lights or in a sunny window, set pots over water-filled trays or trays filled with moist pebbles. When plants are outdoors in the summer months, it is safe to sprinkle them with water on sunny mornings because they will dry quickly in the sun and fresh air. In a greenhouse I use a hose nozzle that provides a fine mist. This increases humidity quickly and leaves a light coating of mist on the foliage without soaking the roots. To discourage rot and fungus attacks on orchids indoors, avoid having water on the foliage at night.

Fertilizing Provide actively growing plants with a water-soluble balanced orchid fertilizer or with a water-based fertilizer such as 7-9-5; mix at half the recommended strength and apply at least once a week. To encourage flowering on mature plants it's best to switch to a lower nitrogen bloom-booster liquid or water-soluble fertilizer in the fall. Use mixes such as 3-12-6 or 10-50-20 at half the recommended concentration. When plants are not making new growth, often directly after flowering, reduce fertilizer applications to once a month.

Potting Angraecoids thrive in well-draining mixtures of coarse perlite with tree fern and bark. For good drainage, place hardwood charcoal and polystyrene in the bottom of the pot. Smaller plants and seedlings do well in plastic pots, especially those with extra side drainage slots. The taller angraecoids are more stable in heavy clay pots. At repotting time pick out rotted mix or gently shake the plant upside down to avoid breaking any roots.

Chunks of hardwood charcoal, tree fern, and coconut husks are good choices for mature angraecoids. Coarse New Zealand sphagnum moss, distributed loosely around the bases of plants, is excellent for seedlings and smaller-growing plants. New Zealand sphagnum moss is especially useful since it lasts several years longer than other types of sphagnum moss.

Cut-Down Popular large-flowered angraecoids such as *Angraecum superbum, A. eburneum,* and *A. sesquipedale* eventually grow three to four feet tall, and the lower stem loses its leaves. To reduce the height of mature plants you can cut the stem just below a set of healthy leaves and several active roots. Do this in late spring or early summer when the plants are actively growing. Always cut the stem below several sturdy roots to make sure that the top

growing section will reestablish quickly. Soak some coarse New Zealand sphagnum moss in a hormone solution, such as Superthrive, then loosely stuff the moss around live roots to help the cut-down plant recover. To save space you can place the active growing tip of the cut-down plant in the same pot with the old base. Be sure to shake out or pick out the old potting mix in the container, but let the roots stay attached to the container and any durable media such as lava rock, pebbles, and crocks. Save the old base, as dormant buds sometimes sprout into new plantlets.

If new shoots do appear, you can encourage them by placing some moist New Zealand sphagnum moss around the base. I make a solution of one teaspoon plant hormone liquid, such as Superthrive, plus half a teaspoon of 7-9-5 fertilizer per gallon of water, and use it to saturate the sphagnum moss. The hormone stimulates new growth, and the fertilizer helps plants get established during the prime summer growing season.

Angraecum White Emblem and many other orchids thrive outdoors during the summer months.

Cattleya Alliance

Ned Nash

At the dawn of modern orchid culture in the mid-19th century, the chance discovery of *Cattleya labiata* in a shipment of plants from an unknown area of Brazil set the horticultural world on fire, and excitement about "the queen of orchids" continues to this day with the significant horticultural achievements being made in Taiwan. No other group of orchids comes in the fantastic range of colors and sizes as the *Cattleya* Alliance. *Cattleya amethystoglossa* and *C. guttata* can reach over six feet, while the dwarf varieties of *Laelia* and *Sophronitis* can comfortably fit into a teacup. The flowers of the largest modern hybrids can reach well over eight inches in diameter, and the range of miniature hybrids—with two- to three-inch flowers that often exceed the size of the plant—just keeps expanding.

Cattleyas beckon with a dazzling palette: whites, with yellow throats or red lips; countless shades of lavender, most with darker lips; yellows ranging from pastel lemon to the most intense gold, many with contrasting red lips veined in gold; all kinds of reds, oranges, and salmon hues; party-colored splash petals with a mixture of tones that can include shades of green and bronze, in some cases even near blue. Beyond the wide range of colors, many cattleyas tempt with fascinating shapes and tantalizing fragrances. Hybridizing has truly reached a pinnacle of

Above: Gardeners in frost-free climates may be able to grow hybrids of *Laelia anceps* outdoors, as the plants are tolerant of near-freezing temperatures. Opposite: One of the largest cattleyas, *Cattleya amethystoglossa* can reach six feet.

Cattleya Slc. California Apricot is a small plant that will thrive in a four- to five-inch pot.

creativity, and today's enthusiasts are its beneficiaries.

Unfortunately, cattleyas are not as widely grown now as in past years. Many of the most famous *Cattleya* breeders have retired or otherwise exited the business, leaving only a few to carry the torch, often with a very focused purpose. Some of the best modern standard cattleyas come from Taiwan. For a good selection of reasonably priced plants from respected growers, you may visit just about any orchid show. Be aware, though, that the selection will most likely originate from only a few nurseries as more and more vendors choose not to create their own hybrids, preferring instead to buy from other sources.

In recent years hybrid *Phalaenopsis* have been eclipsing cattleyas in the public's mind as the prototypical orchids. Mastering the art of *Cattleya* culture is no longer the first challenge for budding orchid enthusiasts. From the years immediately following World War II until the early 1990s, *Cattleya* culture was the standard against which all other orchid culture was measured. "Grow like a *Cattleya*, but with less light" or "more heat" or "slightly more water" and so on were the instructions commonly given to novices.

Traditionally, cattleyas were the epitome of "intermediate" orchids. Since many aspiring orchid growers had a greenhouse of some kind, intermediate conditions (one of the three classic greenhouse temperature ranges, the others being warm, or tropical, and cool) were a great starting point. Once they had mastered cattleyas, the orchids most widely available at the time, growers had no trouble understanding how to adapt *Cattleya* care to other orchids. Today, however, more and more orchid growers are indoor gardeners, who can provide only a limited range of growing conditions. This is one of the reasons for the growing popularity of *Phalaenopsis* and other low-light orchids. Unfortunately, when beginning growers attempt to grow a *Cattleya* like a *Phalaenopsis*—particularly if in a moment of rash enthusiasm they have succumbed to the overwhelming beauty of a standard-size plant—they are doomed to failure. Nevertheless, with just a few modifications of their growing setup and a modicum of good sense, indoor gardeners can succeed very well with carefully chosen cattleyas.

A hybrid of *Brassavola nodosa, B.* Moonlight Perfume inherits its parent's heavenly scent and grows prolifically.

Selecting the Right Size

Proper plant selection with size and habit appropriate for the available growing environment is essential for successful *Cattleya* culture. For most growers, small ("mini-catts") to intermediate-size ("midicatts") plants are best. Savvy breeders know this, and there is a broad array of attractive hybrids and meristems (clones) available from a good range of sources. Look for plants that branch freely and mature at no more than eight to ten inches tall, excluding the inflorescence. If you choose plants in that size range, you will be able to provide good light for them, whether you grow them under lights or on a windowsill; taller plants might not fit under your light setup or will get good light only on one side when set on a windowsill.

Most plants should mature in a four- to five-inch-pot and produce multiple inflorescences per pot. There is a good selection of parents whose progeny will fit the bill, including *Cattleya* Slc. California Apricot, *C.* Blc. Orange Nugget, *C.* Sc. Beaufort, and *C. walkeriana*. *Cattleya walkeriana* is a particularly good parent, as it tends to produce relatively large flowers for its size displayed on multiple inflorescences, and it also imparts a delightful perfume, all lovely qualities to pass on to its offspring. *Laelia pumila* and *Sophronitis coccinea* are two other popular parent species, though *S. coccinea* may need cooler temperatures than can be easily accommodated in the home.

There is also a wide array of smaller-growing plants bred from rupicolous (rock-

growing) laelias that originally came from Brazil. Some of the best-known hybrids are *Laelia* Blc. Love Sound, *L.* Lc. Love Knot, and *L.* Sc. Cheerio, with popular parents such as *L. rupestris, L. sincorana, L. briegerii,* and *L. milleri.* These dwarf plants come in exciting shades of yellows, oranges, and reds, but they may be a little more difficult to grow, as they require careful attention to watering and resent too much water.

The "lady of the night," *Brassavola nodosa,* is an increasingly popular parent owing to its compact stature and exotic flower shape. It gives a heavenly scent to its progeny and grows prolifically. Species such as *Cattleya loddigesii* are useful not only for their relatively compact habit but for their seasonal dominance (hybrids that have a species as one of the parents will often have a very pronounced blooming season similar to that of the species). Avoid hybrids from some of the larger-growing species such as *Laelia purpurata* and the huge Brazilian bifoliate catts. Of course, gardeners living in frost-free areas where they may grow their plants out-of-doors for some or all of the year have a much broader selection available to them, though compact plants are always desirable, no matter where you grow your orchids. Gardeners in areas where cymbidiums thrive out-of-doors year-round should not overlook hybrids from the Mexican *Laelia anceps,* which gives progeny tolerance for near-freezing temperatures and produces flowers that closely resemble standard, classic catts.

Cattleya Seedlings and Meristem Plantlets

Commercial growers who sell at orchid shows will often have actual samples or pictures of the plants they are offering. If you are purchasing a meristem plant, you are getting a clone that will be exactly like the sample or picture. If a seedling is your choice, remember that the sample is only an approximation of what you are likely to get. Hybrids are like children; they will be similar but not identical. Which is better for you? It depends on your gambling instinct. If you like the idea of possibly getting something superior, seedlings are for you; if you absolutely must know exactly what your plant is going to look like, purchase only meristems. Whether or not the meristem plants are significantly more expensive than the seedlings depends for the most part on the grower, but you can expect to pay a slight premium for having the guesswork taken out of the process.

Opposite: Members of the *Cattleya* Alliance, such as *Brassolaelia* Richard Mueller × *Epidendrum schumanianum*, upper right, and *Potinara* Hoku Gem, lower left, require bright light but need to be protected against direct sun during the middle of the day.

Light Whether in a greenhouse or in the home, the most important factor in growing cattleyas is light. The plants need bright light to some sun, with no direct sun in the middle of the day. Place them in an east, shaded south (as with a sheer curtain), or west window in the home, and at 40 to 60 percent full sun in a greenhouse (2,000 to 3,000 foot-candles). Leaves should be a medium green color, pseudobulbs erect and requiring no staking.

Temperatures At night, temperatures should be 55°F to 60°F and during the day 70°F to 85°F. Seedlings should have night temperatures five to ten degrees higher. A 15- to 20-degree temperature difference between day and night is best, especially for mature plants. Provided that humidity, air circulation, and shading are increased, plants can tolerate higher daytime temperatures of up to 95°F.

Water Many factors, such as type of container, temperature, and light determine how much water is required. Seedlings need constant moisture, but mature cattleyas need to dry out thoroughly before they receive water again. If in doubt, compare the weight of a dry pot of the same size and type of mix with a wet pot—light means dry, heavy means wet. If you're still unsure, wait a day or two before watering again. Plants in active growth need more water than plants that are resting. Water below 50°F may injure plants, as will water softened by the addition of salts.

Humidity Cattleyas require 50 to 80 percent humidity. In the home, place the plants on trays of gravel partially filled with water, making sure that the plants do not sit in the water. Air should always be moving around the plants to prevent fungal or bacterial diseases, especially in the presence of high humidity or cool temperatures. In the greenhouse, it's best to use a humidifier to increase humidity. Evaporative cooling increases humidity while cooling the air.

Fertilizing Use a high-nitrogen fertilizer such as 30-10-10 or a similar formulation when growing the plants in fir bark. Otherwise use a balanced fertilizer such as 20-20-20. When in active growth, plants need fertilizer at least every two weeks; when they are not actively growing, once a month is enough. Or apply fertilizer with every watering at one quarter the recommended strength. To prevent the buildup of fertilizer salts, thoroughly flush the plants with clear water every month.

Potting When the rhizome of the plant protrudes over the edge of the pot or the potting medium starts to break down and drain poorly (usually after two to three years), it's time to repot. Do this just before new roots sprout from the rhizome, after flowering, or in the spring. Mature cattleyas are usually potted in coarser potting material than seedlings. Until a plant has at least six mature pseudobulbs, move it to a larger pot rather than divide it. When you divide a

plant, you should have three to five pseudobulbs per division. Select a pot that will allow for approximately two years of growth before crowding the pot. Pile mix against one side of the pot and cut off any dead roots. Spread the firm, live roots over the pile, with the cut rhizome against the side of the pot. Fill the pot with medium, working it in around the roots. Pack firmly and stake if necessary. Keep the plant humid, shaded, and dry at the roots until you see new root growth.

—*American Orchid Society*

Cattleyas and their relatives come in all sizes. Diminutive *Laelia pumila*, opposite, easily fits under lights or on a windowsill. *Cattleya walkeriana*, above, is an intermediate size.

Cymbidiums

Wayne Ferrell

There is little subtlety to the beauty of a modern standard show *Cymbidium*. They stun with three-foot-tall spikes carrying up to 15 large orblike flowers of deeply saturated color. But the modern standard is only one horticultural type in this multibranched genus. From the cascading pure white hybrid *Cymbidium* Mini Sarah 'Pearl Falls' and the indoors-growing, citrus-scented *Cymbidium sinense* to the leafless *Cymbidium macrorhizon*, the genus *Cymbidium* offers an abundance of colors, sizes, and fragrances.

Most of the 44 *Cymbidium* species are distributed throughout Southeast Asia, but some species grow as far north as Korea and as far south as southern Australia. In their native habitats, most cymbidiums grow in the forks and hollows of trees, where plant debris accumulates, or as terrestrials in well-draining soil. The climates in these areas are characterized by monsoonal summer rains during the growing season and cool, dry winters during the flowering season.

Many of the showiest *Cymbidium* species, which are also the easiest to cultivate, come from the subtropical regions of the Himalayan foothills. The frost-free winters and cool summer nights make the cymbidiums growing in these climates well suited for outdoor garden culture in areas such as coastal California. In colder areas, gardeners can bring these species to flower but must move them indoors to a cool but bright location once frost is near.

Above: *Cymbidium* Kusada Fantasy 'Carioca' is a fall bloomer. **Opposite:** *Cymbidium* Mount Airy, a miniature hybrid.

Selecting Cymbidiums

The most spectacular of the species is the autumn-blooming, tiger-striped *Cymbidium tracyanum*. The flowers of this tree- and rock-dwelling species native to Myanmar are bronze-green overlaid with dark red stripes and dots and can measure six inches across. The orchid's wonderful fragrance is as distinctive as its appearance.

The Vietnamese native *Cymbidium erythrostylum* is the first of the large-flowered species to bloom each year. The flowers of this modest-size species are crystalline white with a distinctive "rabbit ear" shape and can open as early as October. Most of the showy species require cool growing conditions, but *Cymbidium erythrostylum* is one that flowers well in the intermediate greenhouse.

For tall, arching flower spikes with lots of long-lasting flowers, there is no orchid that compares with *Cymbidium lowianum*. For this later-blooming species, it is common that the first of up to 30 apple-green flowers on a spike open in March and last in perfection through May. Large-flowered species such as this one are the forebears of the amazing standard show plants winning medals today. For over a century, breeders have thoughtfully, artistically, and patiently sifted the genes of successive generations to produce varieties with very large round flowers in deeply saturated colors.

Cymbidium Maufant 'St. Helier' is one such variety. Bearing 14 rosy-pink flowers on one spike, each measuring nearly six inches across, it received a silver medal from the Royal Horticultural Society. Equally distinctive, *Cymbidium* Hot Port 'Wiki' won an award for its size, deep bronze-red color, and round shape.

The varieties producing these big flowers are large plants, often requiring at least a two-gallon pot to reach their flowering potential. Alternatively, there are many standard varieties with slightly smaller flowers, measuring three to four inches across, that will grow in a one-gallon pot and produce multiple arching spikes with flower counts ranging from 15 to 25. One of the most beautiful of these first flowered three decades ago. *Cymbidium* Mighty Mouse 'Minnie' has up to 25 lovely orange-bronze, three-inch flowers carried on an arching spike.

Cymbidiums With Patterned Petals

If you like stripes, splashes, and dots, you may want to grow some of the novelty varieties. Breeding and fortuitous mutations in the cloning process have created some of the most unusual and beautiful varieties. *Cymbidium* Winter Fire 'Splash' and Pia Borg 'Flash' are two with deep red coloring feathered on all sepals and petals with ice-white. The lovely splash-petaled variety *Cymbidium* Isle 'Flamingo' AD/CSA has

Miniature varieties are typically one to three feet tall with three-inch flowers. Most are easier to bring to bloom than standard-size plants. Left: *Cymbidium* Tiny Tiger. Right: Cascading hybrid *Cymbidium* Mini Sarah 'Pearl Falls'.

burgundy lip markings splashed on its green upper petals. *Cymbidium* Piñata 'SanBar Black Hole' JC/AOS has nearly five-inch beige-yellow flowers uniformly covered with large black-maroon dots.

Miniature Varieties

For growers who look for a compact plant with lots of flowers, the miniature and intermediate varieties are perfect. With an overall height of one to three feet, including the inflorescence, and flowers two to three inches across, these varieties are generally easier to bring to flower than standard-size plants. One miniature that typifies these qualities is *Cymbidium* Autumn Beacon 'Geyserland'. It displays lots of burgundy-colored flowers yet never grows taller than two feet. Slightly larger, *Cymbidium* One Tree Hill 'Solstice Gold' B/CSA has all of the qualities of a good intermediate. The flowers are a vibrant yellow-green with a contrasting dark red bar across the lip; they are well spaced and held high above the foliage. Additionally, the plant produces one to two flower spikes for each new bulb.

With an overall plant height of under one foot, the true miniatures or "teacups" are the smallest cymbidiums. The diminutive plants commonly produce three or four flower spikes each season. The yellow albino *Cymbidium* Wakakusu 'Delight' and the dark pink Minneken 'Khobai' are two of the most prolific bloomers. With teacups it is possible to display a nice collection of cymbidiums on a bench the size of a cutting board.

The use of the miniature Chinese species *Cymbidium ensifolium* in breeding has brought the desirable qualities of fragrance, autumn blooming, and heat tolerance to miniature cymbidiums, which can now be cultivated in southern areas and in the home. And outdoor orchid growers can now expect fragrant cymbidiums in flower as early as August. *Cymbidium* Kusada Fantasy 'Carioca' is a favorite for its mass of fragrant pure yellow flowers. The *Cymbidium* Summer Love varieties lack fragrance but make up for it by producing tall spikes with near standard-size pink flowers that bloom in fall.

Cymbidium ensifolium is an important member of the horticultural group commonly known as Chinese cymbidiums. This group consists of five true miniature species from Asia with delicate flowers that are delightfully fragrant. These species may require slightly more care than other types of cymbidiums, but most will do well with intermediate conditions. Among the most fragrant and easy to grow are *Cymbidium ensifolium, C. sinense,* and *C. goeringii.*

Cascading Hybrids

If there were to be a current craze in *Cymbidium* growing and hybridizing, it would have to be cascading varieties. These bloom as profusely as other miniatures, but they have pendant flower spikes. They grow equally well on a bench or in a hanging basket but are displayed best when elevated to allow room for flower spikes that range in length from 6 to 30 inches. One of the most floriferous is the albino *Cymbidium* Sarah Jean 'Ice Cascade' AD/CSA. As this variety grows to specimen size, it often has so many flowers that the pot cannot be seen behind the froth of white flowers. *Cymbidium* Nicole's Valentine 'Geyserland' HCC/AOS produces a striking display of cascading dark burgundy-purple flowers. *Cymbidium* Dorothy Stockstill 'Forgotten Fruit' AM/AOS is distinctive for its high flower count, up to 35 cinnamon-colored flowers on a single 20-inch inflorescence.

For gardeners who can't provide cool growing conditions, there are cascading species from tropical and subtropical areas that will flower in an intermediate greenhouse. The green- to bronze-flowered *Cymbidium finlaysonianum* is one; *C. atropurpureum* is another, with dark maroon flowers and a coconut scent.

Cascading varieties are the current craze in *Cymbidium* breeding. These bloom as profusely as other miniatures but have pendant flower spikes. Opposite: *Cymbidium* Green Cascades.

Light This is the most important factor for growing cymbidiums. Without proper light you will see weak growth and no flowers. Mature plants require 55 percent shade. Filtered light all day or full morning sun is the rule. Foliage should be yellowish-green in color. Too much light will result in pale yellow leaf color. If a leaf gets burned, you will notice a black spot at its arch. If severely burned, the leaf will be bleached white.

Temperatures Ideal temperatures are under 90°F and above 40°F. The plants can tolerate 32°F but should receive some protection if the temperature drops further. Damage to spikes will occur at 27°F and to the plant at 25°F. To guard against the effects of cold, move cymbidiums against a protected wall or under a tree, or, if you live in a climate with cold winters, move the plants into the house when frost is near. Bright filtered light and indoor nighttime temperatures in the mid-50s will ensure healthy flower development.

The difference between day and night temperatures in fall plays a key role in the development of flower spikes. If nighttime temperatures go above 58°F to 60°F for any extended period of time in fall the buds may turn yellow and drop off.

Water Generally water once a week in winter and twice a week during the heat of summer. Of course, extended periods of dry heat, winds, rain, and/or cold will alter the plants' requirements. One rule remains constant: Water thoroughly each time. Water once to wet the mix and once again to drench the roots. The coarser the medium, the more often you will have to water.

Humidity Cymbidiums do not require too much humidity to thrive—40 to 50 percent is usually sufficient. During hot spells humidity in the greenhouse can be boosted by misting down the plants and the surrounding floors and benches. For plants that have been moved indoors for the winter, humidity provided by humidifiers, nearby kitchens, and bathrooms is helpful.

Fertilizing Provide fertilizer throughout the year since the potting medium provides very little. Use a well-balanced fertilizer, such as 20-20-20, once a week at half the strength recommended on the label. Or apply a time-release fertilizer, such as Osmocote 17-6-10 with trace elements, once a year.

Potting Cymbidiums grow best in $\frac{1}{8}$- to $\frac{1}{4}$-inch fir bark. Every three to four years, when the potting mix has decomposed or the plant is growing over the sides of the pot, it is time to repot and/or divide a *Cymbidium*.

To do so, first take the plant out of the pot and remove the old bark. If you decide to divide the plant, look for natural divisions that allow three- to five-bulb groupings. Remove the dormant bulbs (back bulbs) if you can do so without destroying the strength of the division. Pot the dormant bulbs and you should see flowers in three to five years.

Select a new pot that will allow the plant to grow unrestrained for three to four years. Usually, two inches between the plant and the side of the pot are sufficient. Before placing the plant into the pot, remove any roots that have died or flattened out. (Remember to disinfect the cutting tool before using it to work on another plant.) As you place the plant in the pot, position the bulbs so that they are partly submerged into the medium (about one quarter of the bulb). Be sure that the newest growth is in the center of the pot, which will allow the plant to stretch across the pot. After you pour the fir bark around the roots, firmly tap the sides of the pot and then push down with your thumbs on the top of the medium to make sure the plant is firmly in place.

—*Santa Barbara Orchid Estate*

Light is the most important factor in growing cymbidiums successfully: Filtered light all day or full morning sun is the rule. Opposite: *Cymbidium* Balkis × *Cymbidium* George Lycurgas. Above: *Cymbidium sinense* 'Chin Hua Shan'.

Dendrobiums

Thomas W. Purviance and John F. Salventi

One of the largest genera in the orchid family, *Dendrobium* comprises more than 1,000 different species; according to some botanists' estimates, there may be as many as 1,400. There are miniature dendrobiums with solitary flowers less than a quarter of an inch in diameter, and there are plants that are measured in feet, with sprays of four-inch flowers. Dendrobiums range in color from blues to flaming reds, and many are very unusual in shape. Despite all the variation, *Dendrobium* flowers are quite consistent in structure and are easily identifiable: They all have a prominent "chin," which is formed by the fusion of several flower parts.

As with other large genera, *Dendrobium* species can be found in diverse habitats, from tropical to very cool. The greatest number of species occur in the Himalayan region, the Malay Archipelago, New Guinea, Australia, and the islands of the western Pacific. A few hail from Sri Lanka and the Indian subcontinent, Japan, Taiwan, New Zealand, and the Society Islands. Almost all are epiphytic, but there are a few terrestrial species. The diversity of *Dendrobium* habitats is reflected in the wide range of growing conditions in which various species thrive. And since it can be

Like many dendrobiums, these are native to Southeast Asia. Opposite: *Dendrobium pulchellum* 'Dorothy'. Above: *Dendrobium fimbriatum* var. *oculatum*.

tricky to emulate in cultivation the seasonal changes some dendrobiums experience in their natural habitats, many have been categorized as difficult to grow.

Diverse Dendrobiums

Ever since British explorers first began collecting orchids in the mid-1700s, dendrobiums have been taxonomically confusing. Botanists divide the genus into closely related groups using the terms subgenus and section, while orchid growers refer to types or groups, mainly in an attempt to organize the plants according to their growing requirements. The groups are usually divided according to a common feature such as the name of the most commonly cultivated species, for example, nobile type, named after *Dendrobium nobile.* They may also be typed by flower detail, for example, spatulata (antelope) type; growth characteristics, for example, evergreen type; or plant structure, for example, nigrohirsute type (black hairs on the stems).

The most widely available group has the most confusing common name: the *Dendrobium phalaenopsis* (Den-Phal) type, which is named after the species *Dendrobrium phalaenopsis,* a parent of many of the cultivars. Whereas many species have short-lived leaves and are described as deciduous—with leaves that last a few months to a year or two on each newly developing growth but are shed as the dry

Den-Phal types of dendrobiums, such as *Dendrobium* Bangkok Queen 'Ito', grow and bloom readily indoors if given bright light and adequate water and fertilizer.

Dendrobium **Lim Hepa** × *Dendrobium* **Darci Mikami is a Den-Phal type. Modern Den-Phal hybrids are available in a wide range of colors, but white, purple, and lavender are most common.**

season approaches—the evergreen Den-Phal type has tough leaves that last for many years, even the life of the plant. They characteristically have a cluster of canes, averaging 15 to 30 inches in length, with green leaves on opposite sides and a flower stem growing upward from the top of the canes. Modern hybrids exist in a wide range of colors, but white, purple, and lavender are most common. Den-Phal type dendrobiums grow and bloom easily in the home, provided they receive bright light as well as adequate amounts of water and fertilizer.

In late winter or early spring there are usually many beautiful examples of the nobile type dendrobiums for sale. These plants have compact canes covered in pairs of brightly colored flowers. They are most appealing and tempting but are somewhat difficult to bring to flower, as *Dendrobium nobile* hybrids need six to eight weeks of cool nights (about 50°F.) in the fall, after growths mature. If fall nights are too warm plantlets rather than flowers will form on the pseudobulbs. Some recent compact *Dendrobium nobile* hybrids are bred to bloom without a period of cool nights, which makes them easier to grow in the home. These include *Dendrobium* Yellow Chinsai (*D*. Chinsai × *D*. *aureum*) and *D*. Spring Dream 'Apollon' (*D*. Constance Wrigley × *D*. Thwaitesiae).

Tips for Growing Dendrobiums

Light The best location is a southern exposure, but in the heat of the summer you may have to provide some protection from midday sun. With air conditioning there may be less need to protect the plants against burning.

Temperatures Not a concern for growing evergreen-type dendrobiums in the home. If you are comfortable (60°F and above), the plants will also be fine.

Water Dendrobiums need to be watered when the potting medium has almost completely dried out. The number of days between watering depends on the size of the pot, the time of the year, the environment in the home, and the type of potting medium. If you are unsure whether it's time to water a *Dendrobium*—wait another day or two. Also note that plants in active growth require more water than plants that are going through their rest period. To water a *Dendrobium,* take it to the sink and run water repeatedly through the pot until the roots are completely wet and the potting medium has been thoroughly saturated. Allow the plant to remain in the sink for a brief time while excess water drains away from the pot. Dry the pot and return it to the growing area. Never allow the orchid to stand in a saucer of water.

Humidity Dendrobiums need 50 to 60 percent humidity. In the home, place them on trays over moistened pebbles. In a greenhouse, use a humidifier if conditions are too dry.

Fertilizing It is necessary to fertilize dendrobiums regularly when watering. The best approach is to feed "weakly, weekly." Approximately once a week, after thoroughly watering the plant, drench the pot with water to which a balanced fertilizer, such as 20-20-20, has been added.

Potting To sustain and enjoy a *Dendrobium* for many years, it's necessary to repot the plant every 18 months to two years. Most potting media are organic and decompose over time, retaining water and reducing drainage. To keep the root system healthy, remove the old medium completely and add new orchid mix so that water can flow easily and freely through the pot. When potting a tall evergreen *Dendrobium,* pack the medium tightly into the container so that it firmly anchors the tall canes. Don't be afraid to damage the roots. It is essential to have the plant firmly in place.

Dendrobium chrysotoxum requires bright light in winter for good flowering. Opposite is the cultivar 'Hilde'.

Oncidium Alliance

Charles Marden Fitch

Fortunately for indoor orchid growers, the many related genera in the *Oncidium* orchid group have been successfully crossed to produce adaptable multigeneric hybrids with showy flowers. In my collection the most adaptable types thrive with medium light intensity, alongside cattleyas and *Phalaenopsis*. Night temperatures of 60°F to 65°F and humidity between 60 and 70 percent suit this group. Most important for home culture are *Brassia, Miltonia, Odontoglossum,* and *Oncidium.* You will find these genera, and hybrids derived from their showy species, offered by commercial growers around the world.

Brassias

Brassias are worth growing for their abundance of graceful, lightly scented flowers held on arching stems. Some of the hybrids bloom two or three times per year as new growths mature. Brassias are adaptable, easy-to-grow orchids that do well in a mixed orchid collection.

Brassia species are native to tropical areas, including Jamaica, Central America, and tropical South America. One species, *Brassia caudata,* is found in the semitropical Florida Everglades and also in warmer areas, such as Panama. *Brassia maculata,* a compact species with rich yellow flowers, comes from tropical Central America. I

Many genera in the *Oncidium* Alliance have been crossed to produce indoor-growing hybrids with showy flowers. Above: *Beallara* Peggy Ruth Carpenter 'Morning Joy'. Opposite: *Odontoglossum* California.

found sturdy plants thriving on coffee bushes (*Coffea arabica*) in the plantations around central El Salvador at elevations of about 1,300 feet to 2,600 feet.

These brassias receive bright light and, depending on the season, intermediate to warm temperatures. During relatively dry months from November into April these epiphytic orchids can survive weeks without rain. A clone of *Brassia maculata* from El Salvador grows well in my collection under the same conditions used for cattleyas, with nighttime temperatures between 60°F and 65°F. It blooms from summer into fall.

Hybrids, even primary hybrids between two *Brassia* species, are even more adaptable to variations in temperature and light. Recent primary hybrids combine several large-flowered species to produce adaptable offspring. *Brassia* Edvah Loo (*B. longissima* × *B. gireoudiana* var. *majus*) blooms in the fall and often again in midwinter; *Brassia* Edvah Loo × *B. ochraleuca* has delicate, almost lacy flowers that smell like cloves; *B.* Lance (*B. caudata* × *B. gireoudiana*) is a compact plant that produces arching sprays of nine- to ten-inch-long flowers from fall through midwinter.

The adaptable Central American *Brassia verrucosa* and the similarly large *B. gireoudiana* make the primary hybrid *Brassia* Rex, often used as a parent in modern hybrids. *Brassia* Memoria Fritz Boedeker (*B.* Rex × *B. arcuigera*) blooms in spring; *B.* Memoria Walter Bertsch (*B.* Rex × *B. maculata*) has nine- to ten-inch flowers in early spring and often again in fall; *B.* Santa Barbara (*B.* Rex × *B.* Edvah Loo) grows into a vigorous clump that easily fills a ten-inch pot; in spring it gives rise to 15-inch-long flowers.

Miltonias

The popular *Miltonia* hybrids derived from cool-preference species from the Andes Mountains were recently reclassified by taxonomists into the genus *Miltonopsis*. You will still find hybrids, including those derived from showy species such as *Miltonopsis phalaenopsis, M. roezlii,* and *M. vexillaria,* listed under *Miltonia* in many catalogs. Their popular name "pansy orchid" refers to the flat flowers with bold splashes in contrasting colors.

Hybrids between *Miltonopsis* and warmer-growing genera, such as *Brassia* (which produces the genus *Miltassia*), *Oncidium* (which produces *Miltonidium*), and the Brazilian *Miltonia* species such as *M. regnellii* and *M. spectabilis,* are better suited to growing in the home. The Brazilian types adapt more easily to low humidity and high temperatures than the Andean types. Vigorous hybrids that often bloom

Hybrids of Brazilian miltonias that thrive with intermediate temperatures include *Miltonia* Lanikai (*M.* Victoria × *M.* Minas Gerais), at left, and *Miltonia* William Kirch (*M. bluntii* × *M. regnellii*), at right.

throughout the year include *Miltonia* Goodale Moir (*M. flavescens* × *M. clowesii*) and *M.* William Kirch (*M. bluntii* × *M. regnellii*).

Miltonidium, hybrids of *Miltonia* with *Oncidium*, and *Miltassia*, hybrids between *Miltonia* and *Brassia*, are also very adaptable. The complex genus *Aliceara* combines *Miltonia*, *Brassia*, and *Oncidium* to produce vigorous hybrids like *A.* Mervyn Grant (*M.* Star Fighter × *O. crispum*). *Beallara*, a combination of *Brassia*, *Miltonia*, *Cochlioda*, and *Odontoglossum*, has produced some hybrids that have bold contrasting color splashes and flat flower form similar to the cool-growing Andean miltonias. An example is *Beallara* Peggy Ruth Carpenter 'Morning Joy'.

Miltonia warscewiczii is an excellent parent, passing its compact growth and clusters of curly-edged white and maroon flowers to its offspring. It has been used to create sturdy plants offering a big flower show displayed on branched arching inflorescences: Look for *Miltonidium* Pupukea Sunset (*Miltonia warscewiczii* × *Oncidium cheirophorum*) or one of its offspring, *Colmanara* Space Race (*C.* Sphacetante × *Miltonidium* Pupukea Sunset). Some hybridizers, such as former American Orchid Society president Milton Carpenter, have created complex adaptable hybrids that thrive in intermediate temperatures and produce flowers resembling those of cool-growing species.

Odontoglossums

The most famous *Odontoglossum* species are large-flowered plants from the cool Andes such as the round-flowered *O. crispum*, which is widely used as a parent in hybridizing. When orchid growing became a hobby in Victorian England, cool-growing odontoglossums were very popular, but in modern heated homes these plants do not thrive. Recently hybridizers have combined cool-growing species with species that thrive in intermediate or warm conditions. The resulting hybrids are more adaptable, growing well with night temperatures of 60°F to 68°F. One example that's available as a tissue-propagated plant is *Degarmoara* Hani 'Star of Unicorn' AM/AOS (*Miltassia* Charles M. Fitch × *Odontoglossum hallii*). It produces four- to five-inch purple flowers on a sturdy three-foot inflorescence.

Modern hybrids derived from *Lemboglossum* (*Odontoglossum*) *bictoniense* are very suitable for home culture. They thrive with intermediate temperatures and provide a dramatic display of flowers on a branched upright inflorescence. *Odontocidium* Golden Trident 'Sunshine' (*Odontoglossum bictoniense* × *Odontocidium* Hambuhren), for example, is a select tissue-cultured clone with long-lasting yellow flowers. A pure species worth growing for its five- to seven-inch long-lasting, waxy yellow and brown flowers is *Odontoglossum* (*Rossioglossum*) *grande,* originally from Guatemala and mountainous regions of Mexico.

Oncidiums

The genus *Oncidium* includes miniature plants and giant species that form clumps three to four feet across. Temperature preferences range from cool to warm. Their foliage varies from grasslike to succulent. The stiff succulent foliage of some species gives them the popular name mule ear oncidiums.

Best suited to home culture are mule ear *Oncidium splendidum,* with stiff upright chrome yellow flowers and *O. lanceanum,* with fragrant yellow, brown, and pink flowers. Miniature succulent types, called equitant oncidiums (*Tolumnia*), need bright light to do well. These are often cultivated on chunks of cork bark. They grow four to six inches tall, and their foliage is arranged in a fan shape. Sprays of flowers vary in color from white to yellow to red, many with darker markings.

Golden Shower Oncidiums

Oncidiums with sprays of glowing yellow flowers are excellent choices. Several hybrids have gained international fame as long-lasting cut flowers. The sprays of one- to two-inch flowers provide a show for three to four weeks, often twice a year. Superior clones of modern hybrids are widely available as meristem propagations.

You will find yellow spray oncidiums in the offerings of many commercial orchid growers, and you may even see pots of flowering oncidiums at your local supermarket, but the latter will probably be without name tags. *Oncidium* Aloha Iwanaga 'Dogashima' (*O.* Goldiana × *O.* Star Wars) has large flowers on a branched inflorescence. *Oncidium* Goldiana (*O. flexuosum* × *O. sphacelatum*), an older hybrid, easily grows into a clump, producing flowers from spring through summer. *Oncidium* Gower Ramsey (*O.* Goldiana × *O.* Guinea Gold) is one of the most floriferous and vigorous hybrids and very popular as a cut flower. My plant blooms in the fall and often again in summer. *Oncidium* Golden Shower (*O.* Palolo Gold × *O.* Boissiense) has one-inch flowers on graceful, slightly arching inflorescences, usually several times per year. *Oncidium* Sum Lai Woh 'Jungle Queen' (*O.* Goldiana × *O.* Kanoa) usually blooms in the fall with 36- to 38-inch arching inflorescences. A hybrid of *Oncidium* Sum Lai Woh × *O.* Kensei has 1³/4-inch chrome-yellow flowers that resemble an extra-big *O.* Gower Ramsey. *Oncidium*

Top: *Odontocidium* **Golden Trident 'Sunshine' thrives in intermediate temperatures and produces long-lasting yellow flowers.**
Above: *Oncidium* **Golden Shower produces flowers on graceful arching inflorescences several times a year.**

Taka 'H & R' (*O.* Goldiana × *O.* varicosum) is an excellent plant, combining compact growth and a branched 20-inch-tall inflorescence. The flower display measures 15 inches by 12 inches around. It is composed of ten branches covered with 1¹/4-inch by 1¹/2-inch flowers. My plant blooms in the spring and again in early winter.

For a spray-flowering *Oncidium* in a different color, consider the chocolate-scented *Oncidium* Sharry Baby 'Sweet Fragrance' AM/AOS (*O.* Jamie Sutton × *O.* Honolulu). The plant produces a branching two- to three-foot-tall inflorescence covered with white-lipped red flowers that last several weeks in perfection. It will thrive in a sunny window, sunroom, or greenhouse with nighttime temperatures around 65°F.

Light Young plants prefer filtered or diffused light of approximately 1,500 to 2,500 foot-candles. Mature plants need between 1,500 to 4,000 foot-candles. Inside the home, a bright windowsill with indirect light is usually adequate. A good indication of proper light is the color of the leaves; they should be light green as opposed to dark green (too much shade) or reddish green (too much light).

Temperatures Most *Oncidium* species and hybrids tolerate temperatures from 55°F to 95°F. In general, hybrids are more adaptable than species.

Water How often the plants need water depends on light, air movement, humidity, potting media, and type of pots involved. Most *Oncidium* species and hybrids prefer a slightly moist medium that provides excellent drainage. They resent drying out completely and are equally resentful of soggy conditions. They usually need more water when making new growth and less once the pseudobulbs have been formed. Water copiously whenever you give the plants water. Be sure to wet the potting medium thoroughly, which also helps reduce the buildup of minerals.

Humidity In their native habitats many *Oncidium* species enjoy relatively high humidity during most of the year. In cultivation, mature species and hybrids require between 50 and 90 percent humidity; seedlings usually prefer 70 percent or more. Generally speaking, humidity needs to go up as temperature, light intensity, and air movement increase.

To raise the humidity level, mist the plants or damp down the greenhouse floor periodically. However, do not mist the plants in the afternoon, as the foliage is more susceptible to fungal and bacterial

infection if it's not dry by nightfall. In the home, place the plants on saucers filled with small pebbles and water to increase the humidity around the plants. Be sure the bottom of the pot is above the level of the water.

Good air movement around the leaves and the bottom of the pot is helpful, as gentle leaf movement reduces leaf temperature; in this way plants tolerate higher light intensity and grow more vigorously. Air movement also helps reduce fungal and bacterial infections, which high humidity alone might otherwise promote.

Fertilizing Moderate feeders, oncidiums thrive with a balanced fertilizer such as 20-20-20, applied at one half strength at every second or third watering. If the plants are potted in fir bark, a high-nitrogen fertilizer such as 30-10-10 will be required because the bark extracts nitrogen from the mix as it breaks down. Generally, increase fertilizer applications during warmer weather and when plants are in active growth; reduce them during the cooler months.

Potting Oncidiums need to be repotted about every two years. Plants growing in spaghnum moss may need to be repotted every 12 to 18 months, as this excellent medium tends to break down in that time. Plants grown in inorganic material, such as rock wool or perlite, or those mounted on cork bark or tree fern slabs should be repotted only when the plant has outgrown the pot or slab.

Usually oncidiums should be repotted when the new growth is two or three inches tall or when the new roots first appear. Gently take the plant from the pot, remove any organic media, and trim off all dead roots. Wash the roots gently under running water and then dip them in a dilute fungicide solution. If it is necessary to divide the plant, keep at least three to five mature bulbs together. Try to use a small, shallow pot that allows room for an anticipated one or two years growth. A pot that's too large will hold too much water in the medium and may promote root rot. A pot that's too small will tend to dry out more quickly and may require repotting sooner. Water a newly repotted plant lightly until the new roots have penetrated the medium, then resume normal watering.

Generally, any water-retentive mix that allows for good air movement is suitable. A few good media are spaghnum moss, tree fern, fir bark, charcoal, and all sorts of combinations.

—*Milton Carpenter*

Opposite: *Odontoglossum crispum* 'Charlesworth' AM/AOS. Above: *Aliceara* Mervyn Grant 'Talisman Cove' at left, *Forgetara* Everglades Pioneer at right.

Phalaenopsis

Carlos Fighetti

Without a doubt the most popular orchids today, *Phalaenopsis* are being grown by the millions in Florida, California, Hawaii, and other relatively warm regions of the United States, as well as in Brazil, Costa Rica, the Netherlands, and many countries in the Far East, including Taiwan and Japan. Previously only available at orchid shows and in flower shops, *Phalaenopsis* are now found in most garden centers and even in supermarkets and hardware stores. They are popular because they are relatively inexpensive, easy to grow, and very rewarding. They mature fast, the flowers are nicely displayed above the foliage, and they can bloom for extended periods of time, normally during the winter, but often well into summer.

To make cultivation easier, *Phalaenopsis* are usually divided into five groups. One group includes the species. Then there are three groups of standard-size hybrids: large-flowered white, pink, semi-alba, and candy-striped; novelty hybrids in newly developed colors and patterns, which include reds, oranges, yellows, as well as flowers with spots, bars, and blotches; and multiflora hybrids with an abundance of smaller flowers. And finally there are small-flowered miniature hybrids.

Phalaenopsis species come from an area that includes northern India, southern China, and northern Australia. There are approximately 80 species in the genus,

Phalaenopsis bellina (P. violacea Borneo type), opposite, a beautiful and fragrant species native to Borneo, illustrates the allure of this popular and widely grown genus. There are hundreds of hybrids to choose from, including *Phalaenopsis* Brother Derek (*P.* Brother Fancy × *P. equestris*), above.

which is divided into five subgenera, two of which are further divided into sections. In general, each subgenus and section has its own cultural requirements. The plants are epiphytic, growing on trees, or lithophytic, growing on rocks.

In nature, phalaenopsis are predominantly found in three distinct habitats, with the majority living in constantly moist or humid areas. They are also found in regions with seasonally dry or seasonally cool weather. The challenge in growing *Phalaenopsis* species lies in identifying the plants, determining their habitat requirements, and providing growing conditions to match.

The species native to warm and humid habitats from the subgenus *Phalaenopsis* are easiest to grow and most commonly found in cultivation. They include *Phalaenopsis amabilis, P. aphrodite, P. philippinensis, P. sanderiana, P. schilleriana, P. stuartiana, P. equestris, P. lindenii,* and *P. pulcherrima* (formerly *Doritis pulcherrima*). These plants are also the basis for the majority of hybrids available today, a boon to gardeners, as the hybrids are also easy to grow and require the same type of warm and humid growing environment as their parents.

The second group of species, also found in cultivation, is from the subgenus *Polychilos* and includes *Phalaenopsis amboinensis, P. gigantea, P. lueddemanniana, P. venosa, P. bellina,* and *P. violacea.* These plants also come from a warm and humid habitat. The flowers of these species are brightly colored and have a waxy texture.

The plants in the third group are most difficult to grow. These are miniature species from the subgenera *Parishinae* and *Aphyllae* and include *Phalaenopsis gibbosa, P. lobbii, P. parishii,* and *P. wilsonii.* These plants grow at higher elevations in seasonally cool and dry areas, and they are a challenge to cultivate. They should not be grown together with the other *Phalaenopsis* species because they require cooler and dryer conditions.

Large-Flowered *Phalaenopsis* Hybrids

The most commonly grown *Phalaenopsis,* accounting for more than half of all the orchid plants being produced commercially, are the large-flowered hybrids that growers have propagated by seed or with the help of tissue culture.

White-flowered hybrids like *Phalaenopsis* Taisuco Crane, *P.* Taisuco Kochdian, *P.* Cygnus, *P.* Yukimai, *P.* Sogo Musadian, *P.* White Dream, and *P.* Florida Snow produce long inflorescences covered with up to 20 five-inch flowers. The same goes for pink-flowered hybrids: *Phalaenopsis* Nobby's Pink Lady, *Doritaenopsis* Minho Valentine, *D.* Minho King Beauty, *P.* New Cinderella, *D.* Taisuco Firebird, and *D.* Sogo Smith have many four- to five-inch flowers, nicely arranged on a long inflorescence.

In addition, hybrids with large white flowers and a red lip, commonly called semi-albas, are also available. Two examples are *Phalaenopsis* Luchia Lip and *Doritaenopsis* City Girl. Semi-albas, as well as candy-striped and spotted *Phalaenopsis,* were bred by crossing standard whites or pinks with smaller striped or spotted species. Some attractive candy-striped hybrids are *P.* Sogo Zebra, *P.* Chih Shang Stripes, and *D.* Okay Seven; and some pretty spotted hybrids are *P.* Carmela Spots, *P.* Rousserole, *P.* Soroa Delight, and *D.* Leopard Prince.

Doritaenopsis Yu Pin Angel 'Maria Teresa': A *Doritaenopsis* is a cross between two related genera, *Doritis* and *Phalaenopsis,* which are so close that botanists debate whether *Doritis* should be included in the genus *Phalaenopsis*.

Novelty *Phalaenopsis* Hybrids

Most people who grow *Phalaenopsis* seem to start with whites and pinks and then move on to brightly colored novelties that come in shades of yellow, red, and orange. The quest for novelties started about 40 years ago when a standard white flower or a standard pink flower was crossed with a brightly colored species. The ultimate goal of the hybridizer was to produce brightly hued flowers that have the same shape and size of the whites and pinks. Today novelty flowers are almost as large as the standards, and they have the same round form. Species like *Phalaenopsis amboinensis, P. venosa, P. lueddemanniana, P. pulchra, P. violacea, P. bellina,* and *P. gigantea* were the ones originally used in hybridizing. Today, hybrids of these species are being used to continue the breeding trends to increase the flower size and the number of flowers in the inflorescence; and once in a while the species are used again to intensify the color.

Some handsome yellow-flowered hybrids are *Phalaenopsis* Carol Campbell, *P.* Emil Giles, *P.* Brother Lawrence, *P.* Taipei Gold, and *P.* Golden Bells, *P.* Sogo Manager and *P.* Brother Passat. They all bear five to ten full, rounded flowers on erect inflorescences. Spotted and barred yellows are also available, sometimes from the same parents. *Phalaenopsis* Golden Amboin, *P.* Yellow Queen, *P.* Ching Her Buddha, and *P.* Golden Sun are fine examples.

And then there are the reds. To create a red *Phalaenopsis*, a yellow flower (either a species or a hybrid) is bred to a purple species or hybrid. This results in flowers with diffused pigmentation: Color is evenly distributed throughout the flower, giving the appearance of solid coloration. Shades range from orange-red to deep lavender-burgundy. Some examples are *Phalaenopsis* Cordova, *Doritaenopsis* Lonnie Morris, *P.* Sogo Pony, *P.* Sogo Rose, and *P.* Sogo Grape. In certain hybrids the color pigmentation is concentrated in some areas of the flower, and red spots appear over a yellow- or cream-colored background. *Phalaenopsis* Brother Purple, *P.* Sogo Prince, and *P.* Golden Peoker are a few spotted reds.

Desert tones, or art shade flowers, which include orange, copper, rusty red, or bronze tones, result from the combination of red and lavender color pigment found on the surface of the flower with yellow and green color pigment found inside the flower tissue. The blending of pigments can't be controlled in breeding, and as a result, the progeny come in a broad spectrum of colors. Often the flower colors change as the flowers age, but in some hybrids the pigmentation remains stable and beautiful colors result. Especially noteworthy are *Phalaenopsis* Sweet Memory, *P.* Zuma Aussie Delight, *P.* Pago Pago, and *P.* Brother Sara Gold.

Finally, a new line was recently created in Taiwan, when a mutated form of *Phalaenopsis* Golden Peoker was used in breeding. This resulted in harlequin-type flowers. They have a white or yellow base color and are adorned with randomly distributed large dark, almost black blotches that resemble ink spots. They vary in size and shape and are different from flower to flower, creating very unusual patterns. This can be seen in *Phalaenopsis* Ever-Spring Light, *P.* Yu Pin Pearl, *P.* Yu Pin Panda, and *P.* Bright Peacock.

Multiflora *Phalaenopsis* Hybrids

Multiflora, or sweetheart, *Phalaenopsis* were developed in California by Herb Hager, considered by many as the father of *Phalaenopsis* hybridizing. He focused his efforts on species with large numbers of smallish flowers in each inflorescence. Working with *Phalaenopsis equestris, P. stuartiana, P. lindenii,* and *P. amabilis* var. *formosana,* he created *P.* Be Glad, *P.* Cassandra, and *P.* Vilind. Today, there are quite a few multiflora *Phalaenopsis* available that have all the features Hager had envisioned: smallish plants with a multitude of brightly colored flowers displayed either on several inflorescences or on one branched inflorescence. Examples are *Phalaenopsis* Carmela's Pixie, *P.* Zuma's Pixie, *P.* Timothy Christopher, *P.* Be Tris, and *Doritaenopsis* Quevedo.

Phalaenopsis such as this *P.* Brother Buddha × *P.* Baby Angel 'Talisman Cove' grow easily in a bright window, with little or no sun.

Miniature *Phalaenopsis* Hybrids

This line of breeding is somewhat new, and hybrids are sometimes difficult to come by. Miniature species, such as *Phalaenopsis lobbii* and *P. parishii,* are bred with other small-flowered *Phalaenopsis.* The culture of these hybrids is also somewhat different because the species used in breeding come from cool or dry habitats, and consequently, they require lower day and night temperatures and lower humidity. Some miniatures are *Phalaenopsis* Micro Nova, *P.* Mini Mark, and *Doritaenopsis* Anna-Larati Soekardi.

Light *Phalaenopsis* grow easily in a bright window, with little or no sun. An east window is ideal in the home; shaded south or west windows are acceptable. In overcast, northern winters, the plants may need a full south exposure. It's easy to provide artificial lighting. Place four fluorescent tubes in one fixture supplemented by incandescent bulbs about 6 to 12 inches above the leaves for 12 to 16 hours a day, following natural day length. In a greenhouse, provide enough shade so that the available light is between 1,000 and 1,200 foot-candles. No shadow should be seen if you hold your hand one foot above a plant's leaves.

Temperatures *Phalaenopsis* usually require above 65°F at night and between 75°F and 85°F or more during the day. Higher temperatures force faster vegetative growth, but they must be accompanied by brighter light, humidity, and air movement; the recommended maximum is 90°F to 95°F. To initiate flower spikes, night temperatures to 55°F are desirable for approximately two weeks in the autumn. Fluctuating temperatures can cause bud drop on plants with buds ready to open.

Water As they have no major water-storage organs other than their leaves, *Phalaenopsis* must never dry out completely. Water plants thoroughly, then wait until they are nearly dry before you water again. In the heat of summer in a dry climate, this may be every other day; in the winter in a cool northern greenhouse, it may be every ten days. To prevent rot, water only in the morning, so that the leaves are dry by nightfall.

Humidity The recommended humidity is between 50 and 80 percent. In a more humid climate or in a greenhouse, the air must be moving. Leaves should dry as fast as possible, but always by nightfall. In the home, set the plants on trays of gravel, partially filled with water, but keep the pots out of the water. Fluctuations in humidity can cause bud drop on plants with buds ready to open.

Fertilizing Especially when the weather is warm and the plants are actively growing, it is important to fertilize regularly. Applying a high-nitrogen fertilizer, such as 30-10-10, twice a month is appropriate when bark-based media are used. Otherwise, a balanced fertilizer, such as 20-20-20, is best. In warm weather, apply balanced fertilizer at half strength with every watering; when the weather is cooler or overcast, apply a weaker fertilizer solution twice a month.

Potting It's best to pot *Phalaenopsis* in the spring or early summer, immediately after flowering. They require a porous mix and must be repotted every year. Mature plants can grow in the same container in a medium-grade mix until the potting medium starts to decompose, usually within two years, at which time the plants should be repotted. If the plants are left in a soggy medium. root rot occurs. Seedlings usually grow so fast that they should be repotted in a fine-grade medium every year. To repot, remove the old medium from the roots, trim soft, rotted roots, and spread the remaining roots over a handful of medium in the bottom of a new pot. Fill the rest of the pot firmly with medium, working it in among the roots so that the junction of the roots and the stem is at the top of the medium.

—*American Orchid Society*

Most people who grow *Phalaenopsis* start with the standard whites and pinks, then move on to brightly colored novelties in shades of yellow, red, and orange. Opposite: *Phalaenopsis* Cassandra × *P.* Brother Nugget, an unregistered hybrid. Above: *Phalaenopsis* David Lim.

Pleurothallid Alliance

Cordelia Head and Marguerite Webb

The Pleurothallidinae is a vast and varied subtribe comprised of about 32 genera and more than 4,000 species, with flowers that range from the intricate and bizarre to the showy and sublime. They are widely distributed in tropical America from southern Mexico and Florida to southern Brazil. Spanning a remarkable range in altitude, pleurothallids can be found from the hot sea-level lowlands to alpine elevations above the tree line. However, the majority of pleurothallids occupy moderate altitudes of about 5,500 feet, making them good candidates for intermediate growing conditions in the greenhouse or home.

In nature, pleurothallids grow epiphytically on the lower parts of trees, either on the mossy trunk or the lower branches. Usually their environment is shady and moist. Because most pleurothallids do not require bright light and tolerate a wide range of temperatures, they are well suited for home growers.

Pleurothallids range in size from the tiny ^{1}/8-inch-tall *Barbosella dussenii* to the giant-leafed three-foot *Pleurothallis titan*. The plants may grow as fuzzy vines, mosslike mats, or tufts of tessellated foliage. They may have large *Anthurium*-like leaves, pencil-shaped foliage, or round silvery pendant leaves. Even more exotic and fascinating are the floral possibilities of the Pleurothallid subtribe. Some plants are dwarfed by relatively enormous flowers, and others have tiny blooms that are abundant year-round.

Above: *Masdevallia decumana* 'Danielle' AM/AOS is a miniature orchid with flowers so large they obscure the pot. Opposite: *Masdevallia coccinea* 'Jessica's Delight' HCC/AOS needs protection from summer heat.

Masdevallias

Masdevallia is the showiest and most popular member of the Pleurothallid subtribe. The flower is characterized by fused sepals that elongate into three whimsical tails. The abundance of relatively large, brightly colored flowers makes masdevallias very appealing. At three to eight inches, the majority of the plants are quite compact, which makes it possible to fit a wide variety into a limited space. Many species and most of the hybrids are quite temperature-tolerant and suitable for growing in the home. Choosing plants that are appropriate for your growing conditions is the key to success.

Masdevallia infracta is a hardy plant, ideal for growing in warm to intermediate conditions. The slightly cupped waxy flowers range in color from yellow to lavender to chestnut red. This species is among a group of masdevallias that bloom repeatedly for months on triangular flower stems. As long as the stem remains green the plant may flower again, so do not cut it until it turns brown. *Masdevallia infracta* has been used extensively in hybridizing to promote vigor, warmth tolerance, and continuous flowering.

A Colombian species, *Masdevallia mejiana* has a beautiful white flower with two yellow bands on each side. Each flower is quite long-lasting and has a subtle spicy scent. *Masdevallia mejiana* is an attractive and reliable choice for the warm to intermediate environment. *Masdevallia constricta* is also suitable for intermediate conditions. The unique flower has an elongated sepal tube with a bellylike protrusion. The yellow-orange tails attractively frame the open orange-sherbet throat. *Masdevallia tovarensis* may have up to five crystalline white flowers on each six-inch stem. The pristine beauty, vigor, and warmth tolerance make this plant as desirable today as it was to the Victorians during the orchid mania at the turn of the last century.

The three- to four-inch *Masdevallia strobelii* is encircled with sweet-scented orange and white blossoms filled with soft white hairs. *Masdevallia strobelii* thrives in intermediate conditions, either potted or mounted. This species and others, such as the fabulously fragrant lavender and orange *Masdevallia glandulosa,* so abundantly produce their flowers at the base of the plant that they must be groomed as the flowers fade to avoid the possibility of a fungal infection.

Masdevallia decumana is an example of a miniature orchid with flowers that are so large that they can obscure the plant. Several times a year it produces flat, broad lavender two-inch blossoms. It requires intermediate to cool, moist conditions.

Probably the most eye-catching members of the genus are *Masdevallia coccinea* and its relatives, *Masdevallia veitchiana* and *Masdevallia ignea.* These stately 12-inch plants come from high in the Andes and must have cool, fairly bright conditions to thrive. The most important cultural requirement is protection from summer heat; ideally try to keep below 80°F. *Masdevallia coccinea* is found in an exquisite range of colors, including crimson, fuchsia, hot pink, pure yellow, and white. The flowers stand proudly on tall stems and bloom in late spring and early summer. *Masdevallia veitchiana* is less stressed by summer heat than its relatives, making it easier to grow. The large vivid orange flowers are finely clothed with minute purple hairs, creating a neon effect.

Masdevallia Hybrids

A major trend in *Masdevallia* hybridizing is to make the flashy cool-growing coccinea types more heat-tolerant without losing their vibrant color. Many hybrids possess even greater vigor than their species parents and are excellent choices for the orchid gardener. Hybrids of *Masdevallia infracta* such as the orange and red *M.* Marguerite (*M. infracta* × *M. veitchiana*) and the red to purple *M.* Redwing (*M. infracta* × *M. coccinea*) are temperature-tolerant repeat bloomers with large colorful flowers. *Masdevallia* June Winn (*M.* Redwing × *M. decumana*) produces large, long-tailed rosy-red flowers on medium-size plants.

Masdevallia Copper Angel 'Eichenfels' CCM/AOS is a prolific grower and produces flowers with great abandon.

Masdevallia Angel Frost (*M. strobelii* × *M. veitchiana*) is a tried-and-true hybrid from the early 1980s, which is mass-produced as a pot plant in Japan today. It inherits the free-flowering nature of *Masdevallia strobelii* and has large, slightly cupped lush orange blooms. *Masdevallia* Copper Angel (*M. triangularis* × *M. veitchiana*) is a prolific grower with large, flat copper-orange flowers, which it produces with great abandon. Hybrids of *Masdevallia constricta* have long-lasting waxy flowers. *Masdevallia* Ted Khoe (*M. constricta* × *M. welischii*) has many flowers of polished red-orange, and *M.* Peach Fuzz (*M. veitchiana* × *M. constricta*) bears luscious-looking frosted peach blossoms.

Fragrance is an elusive quality in the genus *Masdevallia,* but it comes to life in a wonderful miniature hybrid called *Masdevallia* Confetti (*M. strobelii* × *M. glandulosa*). The copious pink, white, and yellow flowers emit a strong spicy aroma.

Pleurothallis Species

Pleurothallis ornata (*P. schiedei*), a fascinating orchid from Mexico, has short silver-green succulent leaves and most unusual purple flowers. Small and insectlike, they are edged with a white fringe that moves with the slightest breeze. This miniature

can be grown in bright intermediate conditions. *Pleurothallis truncata* comes from the mountains of Ecuador, where it is found growing in trees and on embankments along roadsides. Many sprays of vivid orange beadlike flowers trickle over each heart-shaped leaf. This ten-inch plant is happy in cool to intermediate conditions either in a pot or mounted on a tree fern plaque.

There are a number of spectacular tall-growing *Pleurothallis* species with large heart-shaped leaves reminiscent of *Anthurium*. The large flowers sit in the middle of the leaves like a frog on a lily pad. *Pleurothallis titan*, native to Colombia, has showy bright yellow flowers; native to Ecuador, *P. teaguei*

Pleurothallis truncata is a native of Ecuador, where it grows in trees and along roadsides.

produces large grapelike clusters of dark purple and white flowers; and *P. gargantua* has hooded burgundy flowers on gray-green leaves. For growers with limited space, *Pleurothallis palliolata* is a good choice. This eight- to ten-inch plant has large striped, dark peach flowers on elongated heart-shaped leaves.

More Species in the Pleurothallidinae

Lepanthes have small, brightly colored flowers and a fascinating variety of foliage. They are all characterized by funnellike bracts along their leaf stems. *Lepanthes calodictyon* has round ruffled-edged leaves tessellated with purple veining. The tiny intricate red and yellow flower nestles like a jewel in the center of the round nickel-size leaves. When given moist conditions and good humidity, this warm-growing species from Ecuador quickly becomes an eye-catching specimen.

Aptly named, *Lepanthes elegantula* has large, one-inch, kite-shaped rich burgundy flowers on wiry arching stems. Flowers appear one after the other over several months, making a lasting and showy display.

One subgenus of *Lepanthes* consists of many vining species. In the wild, chains of round $^1/_4$- to $^1/_2$-inch leaves drip from the branches of low growing trees and shrubs. *Lepanthes platysepala* has relatively flat burgundy flowers of about $^1/_8$-inch. The $^1/_4$-inch flowers of *Lepanthes pilosella* are hooded and brightly striped with red and white. Best grown mounted, these plants are well worth the daily watering needed for good growth.

Restrepias have round paddle-shaped leaves on paper-sheathed stems that grow in compact clumps. Flowers come from the junction of leaf and stem, and each leaf will give rise to flowers for years. *Restrepia cuprea* has beautiful copper-orange flowers; the large-flowered *R. guttulata* has dark rose-pink flowers spotted with purple. The common and floriferous *Restrepia trichoglossa* has sunny yellow flowers striped or spotted with red.

Given high humidity and intermediate to cool temperatures, *Dracula vampira* will flower nearly year-round.

Trisetellas are small grasslike plants that grow in tufts. Showy *Masdevallia*-like flowers appear well above the foliage on thin hairlike stems. Requiring intermediate to cool conditions, the plants thrive in thumb pots and reward the grower with many flowers throughout the year. *Trisetella cordeliae,* from Peru, has large wine-red flowers with yellow tails. The spectacular *Trisetella hoeijeri* has sparkling silvery-pink flowers that appear to be dusted with diamonds.

The genus *Dracula* is characterized by soft green leaves, pendant inflorescences, and hairy monsterlike flowers. They require intermediate to cool temperatures and humidity levels of 80 percent or more. When the humidity is lower, the plants will not flower. The flowers of *Dracula bella* have heavy substance that makes them more tolerant of lower humidity. The large white mushroomlike lip is striking against the yellow-and-red-patterned sepals. *Dracula cordobae,* from Ecuador, has white long-tailed flowers with a red picotee; it grows in warm conditions. *Dracula vampira,* also from Ecuador, is aptly named for its huge sinister-looking purple-black striped flowers. It requires intermediate to cool conditions to produce its stunning flowers nearly year-round.

Light Pleurothallids are not particularly demanding when it comes to light requirements. In cultivation about 1,000 to 1,500 foot-candles is adequate—about the same given *Phalaenopsis* and paphiopedilums. Plants grow well under standard fluorescent fixtures or on an east or shaded south windowsill. Yellow leaves may indicate too much light.

Temperatures Pleurothallids grow in a wide range of temperatures, but for the majority intermediate temperatures are best. Winter nights of 55°F to 60°F are ideal, and maximum summer day temperatures should not exceed 85°F. Cool evenings help reduce the heat stress in the summer.

Water Pleurothallids are sympodial orchids without pseudobulbs for water storage, so correct watering is vital. The plants should be watered often enough to keep the potting medium evenly moist but not sopping wet. Pleurothallids often grow in small pots, so frequent watering is probably necessary. Mounted plants should be watered daily. Overwatering does not compensate for lack of humidity and may cause root rot.

Humidity An important factor in the successful culture of pleurothallids, humidity should be 60 percent or higher. *Dracula, Lepanthes,* and mounted plants have the highest requirement. In the home use pebble trays partially filled with water or a humidifier. Terrariums are ideal for miniatures. In a greenhouse, an evaporative cooler helps raise humidity and lower temperatures. Adequate air movement will reduce leaf temperatures, aid in evaporation (thus increasing humidity),

and reduce the likelihood of disease.

Fertilizing Pleurothallids grow year-round and should be fertilized regularly. They are not heavy feeders. Apply a balanced fertilizer, such as 20-20-20, at half strength twice a month. Overfeeding may cause leaf-tip burn and will accelerate the decomposition of the potting medium.

Potting Pleurothallids require a potting medium that is free-draining yet moisture-retentive. Fine fir bark, medium-grade tree fern and sphagnum moss are widely used. Plastic pots retain moisture. Clay pots dry out faster, but they provide the benefit of cooling roots. Repotting is best done in winter or early spring before the heat of summer. Plants should be repotted every two years before the potting medium decomposes. Pot pleurothallids securely so they will not wobble when watered. The crown of the plant should be positioned level with or slightly above the surface of the medium, never below.

Above: *Lepanthes calodictyon* 'Eichenfels' prefers warm, humid conditions. **Opposite:** *Masdevallia mejiana* 'J & L' is an attractive and reliable choice for warm to intermediate environments.

Tropical Slipper Orchids

Glen Decker

Commonly known as slipper orchids, the genera *Paphiopedilum* and *Phragmipedium* are closely related to the genus *Cypripedium,* the lady slipper orchids, found throughout the world in many northern temperate regions, including North America. Cypripediums grow in the ground and are generally very difficult to cultivate in pots, which makes it virtually impossible to grow them on a windowsill, under lights, or even in a greenhouse. However, paphiopedilums, their Southeast Asian cousins, as well as phragmipediums, their Central and South American relatives, are very well suited for container culture. The cool-growing and warm-growing type paphiopedilums and the phragmipediums are tropical and semiterrestrial. Paphiopedilums are usually found growing in shady locations. Phragmipediums prefer slightly brighter conditions, on forest floors and cliffsides with their roots spreading through layers of moss and leaf litter, but never actually penetrating the mineral soil.

The flowers of slipper orchids have a wide color range, including combinations such as green and white, burgundy and white, pink and white, bronze and white, and tan and white. But much more important than color is the sheer endless variation in flower shapes, with the pouch as the only feature common to all slipper orchids.

Paphiopedilums are slipper orchids native to Southeast Asia. Phragmipediums are their Central and South American cousins. Above: *Paphiopedilum* Dollgoldi 'Laurie Susan Weltz' FCC/AOS; opposite: *Phragmipedium* Living Fire 'Suzanne'.

Paphiopedilums

The *Paphiopedilum* subgenus *Brachypetalum* can be frustrating to grow, yet there are a few beautiful species worth mentioning. It is difficult to keep them from rotting in a greenhouse, as they are sensitive to overwatering and resent getting water in their crowns. However, they like to dry out between waterings, so they do quite well on a windowsill or under lights. Plants worth growing are *Paphiopedilum bellatulum*, *P. concolor*, *P. godefroyae*, and *P. niveum* or any of their hybrids. These plants are the smallest-growing group of paphiopedilums and generally have relatively round flowers ranging in color from white to yellow, usually with spots on their petals.

For an abundance of flowers try one of the sequentially blooming types, such as *Paphiopedilum chamberlainianum*, *P. liemianum*, *P. moquetteanum*, and *P. primulinum*. All the plants in this group can produce several flowers over a course of many months. Wait until the blooming spike actually turns brown and dies before cutting it off, because these may make three or four flowers, stop for a month or two, and then continue to flower.

There are a few others that don't quite fit into the above groups, but they are worth mentioning because they are charming, compact, and easy to grow: *Paphiopedilum charlesworthii*, *P. gratrixianum*, *P. henryanum*, *P. spicerianum*, and *P. tigrinum*. These quickly grow into nice clumps and will bloom with multiple stems of flowers in a rather small pot.

Hybrids such as *Paphiopedilum* Massachusetts Beauty are more tolerant of a gardener's mistakes than species are.

Mottled-Leafed Paphiopedilums

Mottled-leafed paphiopedilums are relatively easy to grow and bring to flower, as they need the least light of all paphiopedilums, doing fine with about 1,000 foot-candles, and thrive in warm growing conditions. In addition, the beautiful mottled foliage makes them quite attractive when they're not in bloom. It is a common feature of slipper orchids but otherwise rare in the orchid world. Provided they are divided every few years, many of the plants stay rather small and compact and are easy to maintain in four-inch-pots. Some species worth trying are *Paphiopedilum acmodontum, P. appletonianum, P. callosum, P. lawrenceanum, P. mastersianum, P. sukhakulii, P. superbiens, P. tonsum,* and *P. wardii.*

Maudiae Hybrids

The Maudiae types are the hybrids of the mottled-leafed group; they also have mottled foliage and are all very easy to grow. There are green and white flowers (album type), dark purple to almost black (vini-color) flowers, or something in between (coloratum type). For flowers with spots, try hybrids of *Paphiopedilum sukhakulii.* My all-time favorite would have to be *Paphiopedilum* Macabre (*P. Voodoo Magic* × *P. sukhakulii*). with its beautiful striped dorsal and spotted petals.

Strap-Leafed or Multifloral Paphiopedilums

The most majestic and expensive paphiopedilums belong to this group. Some seedlings may take as long as ten years or more to mature before they produce their first flowers, hence the price tag. *Paphiopedilum rothschildianum* has tall inflorescences, sometimes reaching two feet in height, bearing three to five very stately flowers, each eight to ten inches across. *Paphiopedilum sanderianum* bears three to five flowers, with petals that can reach three feet or more in length. These species may cost hundreds to even thousands of dollars, mainly due to their desirability and to the time involved to grow them and bring a mature plant to flower. *Paphiopedilum stonei* and *P. philippinense,* also very beautiful, as are many of the hybrids, can be less expensive but may still take many years to grow and bring to flower. Some hybrids to choose from include *Paphiopedilum* Prince Edward of York (*P. rothschildianum* × *P. sanderianum*), *P.* Michael Koopowitz (*P. sanderianum* × *P. philippinense*), *P.* Saint Swithin (*P. rothschildianum* × *P. philippinense*) and *P.* Mount Toro (*P. stonei* × *P. rothschildianum*). These are not sequentially blooming, so once the last flower falls off, it's safe to cut down the flower spike. These orchids all produce about three to five flowers with petals averaging four to ten inches in length, but they tend to grow much larger, some even approaching two or more feet across. These plants are not only large; they also require brighter light and are best grown in a greenhouse.

Fragrant Slipper Orchids

Fragrance is a rare feature in the slipper orchid world and confined to *Paphiopedilum* subgenus *Parvisepalum*. This is a fairly new group of orchids—most of its species were only discovered in the past 25 years. Two that are easy to grow are *Paphiopedilum delenatii,* with pink flowers, and *P. malipoense,* with green flowers. This group enjoys growing in cooler, brighter conditions but will do fine in any growing environment you choose to give the rest of your slipper orchids. Other species in this group, such as *Paphiopedilum micranthum* and *P. armeniacum,* are beautiful, but it can sometimes be frustrating to get them to grow well and bloom. Their cultural needs are very exact, making them difficult even for the most seasoned orchid growers. I find that in my own greenhouse they may only bloom every two to three years. The hybrids are a bit more cooperative and are generally fragrant. Most of the hybrids produce one flower, sometimes two. Some of the hybrids are *Paphiopedilum* Joyce Hasegawa (*P. delenatii* × *P. emersonii*), with white petals and pink pouch; *P.* Lynleigh Koopowitz (*P. delenatii* × *P. malipoense*), with a white flower with maroon tessellations; *P.* Magic Lantern (*P. delenatii* × *P. micranthum*), with pink flowers; and *P.* Harold Koopowitz (*P. malipoense* × *P. rothschildianum*), which can produce three large green flowers with brown tessellations.

Complex *Paphiopedilum* Hybrids

The complex *Paphiopedilum* hybrids are affectionately referred to as toads or cabbages because of the large (up to five inches in diameter), full-shaped, heavy-substance flowers. This group is fairly easy to grow and can tolerate cooler temperatures with any of the light conditions enjoyed by the rest of the slipper orchids. Choosing a plant is strictly a matter of taste: Take your pick among white, yellow, green, red, and spotted flowers. Whereas many people would agree that slipper orchids are graceful, majestic, and pretty, opinion is divided when it comes to the complex hybrids. Sometimes described as hulking, gaudy, and ugly, these plants are usually the domain of the die-hard *Paphiopedilum* fanatic, as it may take time to appreciate their beauty.

Phragmipediums

Phragmipediums have only come back into favor in the last 20 years, due to the discovery of *Phragmipedium besseae,* a beautiful red species native to Peru and Ecuador. Just recently, another new species has come to light in Peru, huge-flowered *Phragmipedium kovachii,* which should boost the popularity of the genus even further.

Many novices as well as some seasoned growers tend to torture their plants with a slow death of under- or overwatering. But this is not that easy to do with phragmipediums, since they love lots of water. They also tolerate a wide range of temperature and light conditions, as you will see from the cultural requirements. Best of all, many of these can bloom for months, bearing eight or more flowers one after the other. The only downside to growing phragmipediums is that many of them can get rather large. A small-growing *Phragmipedium* can grow to be about 12 to 18 inches in diameter, whereas a large-growing *Phragmipedium* may reach three or more feet in diameter, making them a challenge to grow on the windowsill or under lights.

Hybrid Phragmipediums

Until you are familiar with phragmipediums, it's best to stick to the hybrids, because they can tolerate a gardener's mistakes. When growing any species, the idea is to try to duplicate its natural environment, which is not always easy, especially if you are

Some tropical lady slipper orchids are threatened by collectors who dig them up from the wild. Make sure that any species you purchase has been certifiably propagated by seed. Above: *Phragmipedium schlimii* 'Rosa'.

not sure where the plants grow in the wild. Hybrids, however, have what is called hybrid vigor—a wider range of genetic material that allows them to adjust to a wider range of growing conditions. Some of the older hybrids worth a try are *Phragmipedium* Sorcerer's Apprentice (*P. longifolium* × *P. sargentianum*), which will bloom for six to ten months. Another definite favorite of mine is *Phragmipedium* Grande (*P. longifolium* × *P. caudatum*), known for its majestic blooms. It will only produce three to five flowers, but they may last for two months or more, and each flower is very large, with petals that are a foot or more long. The newer hybrids, some of which can be a bit pricey, are all made with *Phragmipedium besseae* and come in a variety of plant sizes and bloom color ranging from pinks to reds to sunset tones. Some of my favorites are *Phragmipedium* Don Wimber (*P.* Eric Young × *P. besseae*), *P.* Elizabeth March (*P.* Sedenii × *P. besseae*), *P.* Hanne Popow (*P. schlimii* × *P. besseae*), *P.* Jason Fischer (*P.* Mem. Dick Clements × *P. besseae*), and *P.* Living Fire (*P.* Sorcerer's Apprentice × *P. besseae*).

Light Paphiopedilums require shady conditions, as in an east or west window in the home, or near a shaded south window. In the greenhouse, give them some shade and provide about 1,000 to 1,500 foot-candles. In the home, fluorescent lighting is excellent; suspend two or four tubes 6 to 12 inches above the leaves. Phragmipediums like slightly brighter conditions, 1,500 to 2,500 foot-candles, but will do just fine grown alongside paphiopedilums.

Temperatures Paphiopedilums are traditionally separated into two groups: the warm-growing mottled-leafed types and the cool-growing green-leafed types. A third increasingly popular group is the warmer-growing strap-leafed multifloral paphiopedilums. Warm-growing types should be kept at 60°F to 65°F during the night, and 75°F to 85°F or more during the day. Cool-growing types should be kept at 55°F to 60°F during the night and 75°F to 80°F during the day. However, many growers raise all plants in the same temperature range with excellent results. The plants can stand night temperatures in the 40s if necessary (as when grown outside in mild climates), as well as temperatures to 95°F. Protect the plants from rot when it's cold (keep humidity low and avoid moisture on leaves or in the crowns of the plants), and protect them from burning when it's hot (shade more heavily and increase humidity and air movement around the plants). Phragmipediums can be grown in any of the above temperature ranges with great success.

Water Slipper orchids have no pseudobulbs, so water must be available at the roots constantly. All paphiopedilums need a moist medium—never soggy but never dry. Water paphiopedilums once or twice a week. Phragmipediums need to be watered every day during the summer months and less frequently during the winter months. If having to water your plants every day sounds like too much trouble, simply place your plants in trays of water. (Probably this goes against everything you have ever been told, but trust me, these plants will love it.) If you continually let phragmipediums dry out, they may never bloom. One word of caution though: Never let the plants sit in water that contains fertilizer. Every time after you fertilize, pour the fertilizer water out of the tray and replace it with fresh water.

Humidity Paphiopedilums and phragmipediums need moderate humidity—between 40 and 50 percent—which can be maintained in the home by setting the plants on trays of gravel, partially filled with water. Never let paphiopedilums sit in water. In a greenhouse, average humidity is sufficient. Using an evaporative cooling system in warm climates can increase the humidity. Air movement is essential, especially when humidity is high.

Fertilizing The plants need to be fertilized on a regular schedule, but be careful not to burn the fleshy, hairy roots. Balanced fertilizers, such as 18-18-18 or 20-20-20, are recommended for both paphiopedilums and phragmipediums. However, during the warmer months when plants are actively growing, you could use a high-nitrogen fertilizer, such as 30-10-10. In warm weather, some growers use half-strength applications every two weeks; others use fertilizer at one quarter strength every time they water. It's important to flush with clear water monthly to leach excess fertilizer, which can burn roots. In cool weather, it's enough to fertilize once a month. Phragmipediums enjoy more fertilizer, and it's best to double the amount of fertilizer recommended for paphiopedilums above.

Potting Plants discussed in this chapter are all easily maintained in four-inch pots, some perhaps requiring a slightly larger pot after several years of growth. The plants should be repotted every two years, or as the medium decomposes. Seedlings and smaller plants are often repotted annually. Mixes vary tremendously; most are fine- or medium-grade fir bark, with varying additives such as perlite, coarse sand, and sphagnum moss. The medium needs to retain moisture well and provide excellent drainage. Large plants can be divided by pulling or cutting the fans of the leaves apart and separating these into clumps of three to five growths. Smaller divisions will grow but may not flower. Spread the roots over a small amount of medium in the bottom of the pot and fill with medium so that the junction of roots and stem is buried half an inch deep in the center of the pot. When selecting a pot for your orchid, make sure that you choose one that is appropriate for the size of the root zone and not the size of the plant itself. It is important that you do not over-pot: If you can fit the roots into a four-inch pot, that is the pot to use. If in doubt, always use the smaller pot.

Hybrids such as *Phragmipedium* Don Wimber (*P.* Eric Young × *P. besseae*) have become popular since the discovery of *P. besseae,* a beautiful red species native to Peru and Ecuador.

Vanda Alliance

David L. Grove

Given the huge number of genera and species in the *Vanda* Alliance, there are vast differences in plant size and floriferousness and in flower color, shape, and size. Some members of the *Vanda* Alliance are very suitable for growing on a windowsill or under lights, while some are so tall when they mature that they present a daunting challenge to anyone who doesn't have a greenhouse or live in a climate that's warm and humid enough for outdoor growing.

While all members of the alliance are monopodial (they grow upward from a single base stem rather than from rhizomes), some remain quite short and compact for a considerable number of years. Others can grow to more than three feet tall, but these can be kept to a more manageable height by severing the plant stalk just below well-established aerial roots and keeping the top section as a new plant. The remaining lower section usually will send out side shoots that can be detached once they have developed roots of their own.

For the most part, *Vanda* species have provided the foundation for the intergeneric hybrids (plants whose ancestry includes species of more than a single genus) in the alliance. The most outstanding of the many intergeneric hybrids in the *Vanda* Alliance is *Ascocenda*, which results from combining species or hybrids of *Vanda* ancestry with ones of *Ascocentrum* ancestry. The combination may be in any proportion, but of course the proportions greatly affect the outcome. Besides *Ascocenda* there are many other popular intergeneric combinations with *Vanda*, such as *Christieara*, a genus name that is applied to hybrids produced by combining members of the *Vanda*, *Ascocentrum*, and *Aerides* genera. Another example is *Vascostylis*,

The most outstanding of the intergeneric hybrids in the *Vanda* Alliance is *Ascocenda*. Opposite: *Ascocenda* Thitapura (*Vanda brunnea* × *Ascocentrum curvifolium*).

which is the genus name of hybrids whose ancestry includes elements from *Vanda, Ascocentrum,* and *Rhynchostylis.*

Some of the man-made genera in the *Vanda* Alliance contain no *Vanda* ancestry at all. Most common are combinations involving *Ascocentrum* species or hybrids, including *Rhynchocentrum,* a genus that combines species or hybrids of *Ascocentrum* and *Rhynchostylis* ancestry, and *Renancentrum,* which combines *Ascocentrum* and *Renanthera* lineages. Then there are some that have neither *Vanda* nor *Ascocentrum* ancestry, such as *Neostylis,* which combines *Neofinetia* and *Rhynchostylis* ancestry. It produces very floriferous hybrids that seldom reach more than 12 inches in height— ideal plants for growing under lights or on a windowsill. The flowers of these compact hybrids can be red, pink, purple, white, orange, or mixtures of colors, depending on their individual parentage.

The Attractions of Species

In addition to the multitude of hybrids in the *Vanda* Alliance, the species themselves offer many delights. The species range from the tall, broad *Vanda sanderiana,* whose racemes each bear eight or more impressive round, flat, bicolored flowers up to five inches in diameter, to the cute half-inch pale lilac blossoms of *Ascocentrum christensonianum,* which are produced on a narrow, rather short plant whose racemes carry about 25 well-arranged flowers. *Vanda sanderiana* is an excellent species for growing in a greenhouse or outdoors in tropical climates, while *Ascocentrum christensonianum*

can be grown just as well under lights or on a windowsill.

Renanthera storei is a tall, striking species with long, arching, branched inflorescences that bear a multitude of vivid red-orange, speckled, star-shaped flowers that delight floral designers. Another species in that genus, *Renanthera monachica,* is substantially scaled down in plant size and has proportionately shorter inflorescences; the flowers are speckled red on an orange or yellow-orange background. While possibly still a bit large for

Opposite: *Vanda coerulea* is one of the *Vanda* species most commonly used in breeding. Above: *Vanda brunnea.*

most gardeners who do not have a greenhouse, *Renanthera monachica* is by no means impossible to grow under lights or on a windowsill. It typically reaches blooming size when it's around 12 inches tall.

Many of the species of nearly all the other natural genera in the *Vanda* Alliance also are excellent plants for hobby growers. Some candidates are *Rhynchostylis coelestis* and any of the species in *Ascocentrum* or *Neofinetia*.

The two *Vanda* species most commonly found in the collections of *Vanda* enthusiasts are *V. sanderiana* and *V. coerulea*. These two species form the platform on which nearly all *Vanda* hybrids and many of the intergeneric hybrids have been constructed. Nevertheless, some other *Vanda* species also are especially well worth growing. Among them are *Vanda tricolor, V. luzonica, V. tessellata, V. denisoniana, V. lamellata,* and *V. cristata.* The flowers of *V. tricolor, V. tessellata,* and *V. denisoniana* offer the special attraction of an alluring heady fragrance. *Vanda cristata* offers an eye-catching lip.

The family trees of the most prized *Vanda* hybrids show far more entries of *V. sanderiana* and *V. coerulea* than of any other species, and other species rarely appear on the family tree of hybrids after the earliest generations. Even then, in the vast majority of instances, only three other species are found: *Vanda tricolor, V. dearei,* and *V. luzonica.* The genes of *Vanda sanderiana* produce hybrid offspring with large, round, flat flowers, and those of *V. coerulea* are responsible for tessellated deep blue flower color. The genes of the other three species contribute red, pink, and clear yellow pigmentation, thereby making possible a multitude of combinations of flower colors and patterns when combined with those of *Vanda sanderiana* and *V. coerulea.*

The Advantages of Hybrids

Most orchid growers prefer hybrids in the *Vanda* Alliance to species, for several reasons. Hybrids offer a much greater variety of flower colors and color patterns and sizes and shapes. Moreover, as a result of generations of selective breeding, the hybrids generally bloom at an earlier age and more often than the species, and they can be grown well in a wider range of environmental conditions. Furthermore, their flowers tend to be somewhat larger, rounder, flatter, and better arranged on their racemes. However, they do not have the fragrance of some of the *Vanda* species.

Within the *Vanda* Alliance, *Ascocenda* hybrids have come to rival in popularity those of *Vanda.* Ascocendas are available in a wider variety of flower colors, shapes, and sizes, as well as plant sizes, depending on the extent of ancestral representation of *Vanda sanderiana* and *V. coerulea.* That combined representation typically ranges from one-half to seven-eighths of the total. The sole *Ascocentrum* species in the ancestry of *Ascocenda* hybrids most often is *Ascocentrum curvifolium*. The plants of this species are short and tend to have numerous side shoots. The species tends to transmit to its *Ascocenda* progeny the red-orange pigmentation of its flowers, pigments not found in the flowers of any of the *Vanda* species. Another fine quality of *Ascocentrum curvifolium* is the round, flat shape of its flowers. By far the best known *Ascocenda* is *Ascocenda* Yip Sum Wah (*Vanda* Pukele × *Ascocentrum curvifolium*).

Some of the less spectacular *Vanda* species that have not been notably successful in the breeding of straight *Vanda* hybrids have produced delightful hybrids when they were combined with *Ascocentrum curvifolium*. For example, *Ascocenda* Thitapura shows the result of combining *Vanda brunnea* with *Ascocentrum curvifolium*. The hybrid is an interesting small plant with star-shaped rich mahogany flowers. More such combinations with less widely used *Vanda* species are becoming available.

Vanda denisoniana has served as a parent of a number of especially attractive and popular *Ascocenda* hybrids with yellow or orange-yellow flowers, often speckled with crimson spots. Moreover, the plants usually are easy to grow.

Most orchid growers prefer hybrids in the *Vanda* Alliance to species because the former generally bloom at an earlier age and more often. Left: *Vascostylis* Crownfox Magic. Right: *Ascocenda* hybrid (*Vanda sanderiana* × *A.* Mildred Furumizo).

Tips for Growing *Vandas*

There are three types of vandas: strap-leafed, terete, and semiterete, and the three groups have somewhat different cultural needs. (Note that there are also terete-leafed orchids unrelated to vandas.)

Strap-leafed plants have flat or V-shaped, leathery leaves. This category includes species such as *Vanda coerulea, V. dearei, V. luzonica, V. merrillii, V. tricolor,* and *V. sanderiana,* as well as ascocentrums.

Terete orchids have tapering, pencil-shaped leaves that are circular in cross-section. The most common vandaceous species in this group are *Vanda teres* and *V. hookeriana.*

Semiteretes are a hybrid combination with some terete species in the background. Their leaves are somewhat pencil-shaped and tapered but not always completely round in cross-section.

Light If the humidity is high, vandas should have maximum sunlight with only enough shade to keep the temperature within the appropriate range and to protect the foliage of strap-leafed plants during the middle of the day. Outdoors, the plants want maximum light without burning the leaves. They benefit from full sun in the morning and late afternoon, but need some shade during the middle of the day.

Terete vandas and their semiterete hybrids are sun lovers. They flower year-round in tropical areas and produce abundant blooms in the subtropics.

Temperatures Vandaceous orchids grow best with daytime temperatures of 65°F or higher, but they can withstand long spells of hot weather and short spells of cold. They will continue in active growth any time of the year if given warm temperatures and bright light. Night temperatures should not generally be lower than 55°F for extended periods. During a period of cold weather, the most important thing you can do is protect the plants from air movement (wind). For the most part, vandaceous orchids need warm temperatures and good air circulation.

The difference between day and night temperatures in fall plays a key role in the development of flower spikes. If night-time temperatures go above 58°F to 60°F for an extended period of time in fall, the buds may turn yellow and drop off.

Water Vandaceous orchids in slat baskets should be watered daily, preferably early in the morning, and then allowed to dry. Water more sparingly in winter, during long cloudy spells, or after repotting. In any season, avoid watering plants late in the afternoon. The plants should be dry before nightfall.

Humidity High daytime humidity is essential, especially on sunny days, and additional misting once or twice a day in bright weather will be helpful. On hot, sunny days around 80 percent humidity is appropriate.

Fertilizing Vandas are heavy feeders. During the growing season, give the plants a solution of a complete, balanced fertilizer, such as 20-20-20, once a week. During the winter (when plant growth is slower), apply fertilizer every two weeks. In addition, substitute a bloom booster, a fertilizer that's high in phosphorus, such as 10-50-10, every third time you fertilize. Do this throughout the year. Avoid high-nitrogen fertilizers, as they will inhibit flowering. Flush the plants thoroughly with plain water once a week to remove built-up salts.

Potting Vandas grow well in any porous medium if it is properly aerated. Tree-fern chunks, coarse bark, or charcoal are good choices. The roots should not be smothered by tight potting or a soggy medium. Wooden baskets with little or no additional growing medium are best, but pots can be used if they provide good drainage. Teakwood is the best choice for baskets, as it lasts the longest. If teakwood is not available, redwood is a good second choice, and cedar a third option. Pot seedlings loosely in a mix of fine charcoal and tree-fern fiber, and keep them in slightly more shaded conditions than mature plants. Use three-inch baskets for the first two years, six-inch baskets for the next two years, and eight-inch baskets for mature plants. Suspend the plants so that the aerial roots hang free; otherwise, the roots attach themselves to the bench or wall and are damaged when the plants are moved. Keep recently potted plants in slightly more shaded conditions until they are established.

Because vandas have large aerial roots, they don't like to be disturbed. So instead of removing them from their smaller, older baskets at repotting time, move them with their old basket into a new one. Soak the roots briefly in water until they become pliable, and then work the roots through the slats of the larger basket so that you can set the plant with its old basket intact into the larger basket. Never coil the roots around the old basket, as vandaceous plants will feed better with an unrestricted root system. Use a few large pieces of charcoal to hold the smaller basket securely within the larger one; or wire the

smaller basket into the larger one. This method minimizes shock to the plant and allows continued, uninterrupted growth. Adding Superthrive or another plant vitamin product to the water used for soaking further minimizes shock and seems to encourage faster growth of new roots.

There are occasions, however, when disturbing the roots cannot be avoided, for example when a basket has rotted or when a pot-grown plant needs to be moved to a larger container. Soak the plant in plain water for a few minutes, and then remove it from the old container as carefully as possible. It may be necessary to dismantle the old basket by cutting its wire fasteners. Clean debris from the roots and soak them in a plant vitamin and fungicide solution for about five minutes, and then move the plant into a new basket or pot. If you must trim roots or leaves, be sure to sterilize the cutting tool. Late spring to early summer is the best season for potting or repotting vandas, but these orchids may be repotted at almost any time of the year.

—R.F. Orchids

Vandaceous orchids generally need warm temperatures and are heavy feeders. Above: *Christieara* **Renee Gerber (***Ascocenda* **Bonanza × *Aerides lawrenceae*).**

Adaptable Miniatures

H. Phillips Jesup

Orchid horticulture in the last century was largely concerned with orchids of imposing size. These familiar types were derived from relatively few species in a handful of genera. Despite the public conception of the flamboyant orchid, the fact is that among the approximately 30,000 species of orchids, the majority are small in plant size, flower, or both, and growers who have space limitations or who are simply intrigued with small things will find a wealth of miniature orchids to choose from. Some have showy flowers so large they nearly obscure the plant that bears them, others have an abundance of small flowers, and some sport an element of whimsy.

As is true of orchid species in general, the miniatures have evolved under a wide range of ecological conditions, from high mountain to sea level near-desert; cool cloud forests to lowland jungle; fully exposed lichen-covered rock faces to shaded, mossy tree trunks. Often the plant form gives a valuable clue to habitat, and therefore, to culture. Prominent pseudobulbs and thick or pencillike (terete) leaves function as water-storage organs and denote brightly lit habitat with relatively low rainfall, at least at a certain season of the year. Broad, thin leaves and pseudobulbs that are vestigial or absent indicate habitat with a uniformly high level of moisture and shade. Culture should follow accordingly. In the home, a sunny win-

Miniature orchids require more vigilance than their larger cousins: Small pots dry out faster than large, and small mounts need more frequent misting than larger ones. Above: *Oncidium cheirophorum.* Opposite: *Cattleya luteola.*

dow would best suit *Leptotes bicolor* or *Oncidium onustum,* while a Wardian case exposed to good light but no sun, and with the top tipped up for ventilation, might provide optimum conditions for cloud forest denizens and *Aerangis rhodosticta.*

Are miniature orchids more demanding than their larger cousins? The answer is a qualified yes. While the cultural conditions for orchids from similar habitats are essentially the same regardless of size, miniatures require closer attention. Small pots dry out faster than large, and the cork, branch, or tree fern mounts for some need frequent watering or misting because the small roots, exposed to the air, dry quickly. A miniature plant with a problem will usually succumb much faster than a larger one, since it takes only a few mealybugs or scale insects to suck much of the life juices from a tiny plant compared with hordes for a large orchid. Vigilance is important.

The species described below represent but a tiny fraction of the fascinating forms available in small orchids. All are adaptable to home and greenhouse culture within the ranges of their tolerance. They are from two to eight inches in height, except for a couple of the oncidiums, which are vegetatively small but have bloom spikes up to 20 inches long. Species are listed in order of their temperature requirements, beginning with the warmer growers.

Warm-Temperature Miniatures

Aerangis rhodosticta has a short, horizontal spray of $1^{1}/_{2}$- to 2-inch narrow leaves with bilobed tips, from which emerges a bloom spike on the same plane bearing six to ten or more $1^{1}/_{4}$-inch flat flowers that face upward in a double rank. They are pure white with a prominent orange dot in the center. This is a shade-growing twig-orchid from Kenya and Cameroon that will grow best with good humidity on a small cork slab or cut section of a rough-barked limb.

Ascocentrum miniatum is a sun lover. A double row of heavy, stubby leaves marked with dark dots clothe a slowly elongating upright stem. Each spring one or two four- to six-inch "candles" of brilliant, closely packed half-inch orange-yellow flowers arise from the leaf axils. The white aerial roots are as thick as pencils and as rigid. This Far East species should grow well in a bright spot in the greenhouse, on a south-facing windowsill, or close to the lights in an artificial light setup. A related species is *Ascocentrum pumilum* (intermediate or cold-growing), which is but $1^{1}/_{2}$ inches high, with needlelike leaves and tiny pink flowers.

Phalaenopsis equestris is a dwarf relative of the larger "moth orchids." It produces a cloud of small rose-pink flowers with darker lips that appear to float on branched

Ascocentrum miniatum, left, is a sun lover, while **Aerangis rhodosticta,** right, grows in shade.

flower stems above three to five broad, flat leaves at the base of the plant. This one is a bit larger than most of the species discussed and is easy to grow under the same conditions of warmth, shade, and moisture suitable for African violets.

Intermediate-Temperature Miniatures

Cattleya luteola is a dwarf, somewhat creeping species. Its thick, paddle-shaped leaves and pseudobulbs total about six inches and resemble a scaled-down version of the familiar (and not very aesthetically pleasing) *Cattleya* growth habit. Clusters of three to eight yellow to greenish-yellow, $1^{1}/_{2}$- to 2-inch flowers erupt from a sheath at the top of the pseudobulb in the spring. The lips are marked with red. This species, found in Peru and Bolivia, prefers a resting period with reduced water after flowering and requires bright light with some sun to flower well. Pots or mounts suit it equally, but do not overwater pots.

Also in the *Cattleya* tribe but quite different in appearance are *Leptotes bicolor* and *L. unicolor.* Both have pencillike round leaves, the former producing several spidery two-inch white flowers with magenta lips, and the latter uniformly pale lavender flowers about half that size. The leaves of *Leptotes bicolor* are three to four inches in length, while *L. unicolor* is a miniature version of its merely dwarf cousin. *L. unicolor*'s rough-textured leaves and its flowers both grow straight downward. For this reason, it should be grown only on a mount. If the plant is attached incorrectly with leaves pointed skyward, it will

The four-inch flowers of *Laelia pumila* seem enormous coming from a six-inch plant. Above: *Laelia pumila* 'Angel'.

remedy that mistake, as subsequently grown leaves will head sharply down. Both of these Brazilian species need bright conditions and not much water at the roots.

Laelia pumila is yet another *Cattleya* relative from Brazil, resembling a dwarf version of a standard lavender florist's *Cattleya*. The four-inch flower seems enormous coming from a plant about the size of *Cattleya luteola,* and it sometimes outdoes itself by producing two such immense flowers simultaneously from a single growth. Pot or mount culture suits it equally, but the somewhat creeping rhizome lends itself better to a slab of tree fern fiber; it will quickly "walk" over the edge of a pot. Strong light but a less pronounced rest than *Cattleya luteola* will induce flowering.

In the genus *Laelia* are a number of very tiny species that grow in declivities on the exposed rocky summits of several Brazilian mountain ranges. They, along with some larger relatives, are collectively known as rupicolous (rock-dwelling) laelias. Species such as *Laelia bradei, L. longipes,* and *L. lilliputana* have butter-yellow, white, and lavender flowers respectively and make entrancing pot plants. Their pseudobulbs resemble green or reddish bullets or marbles, and the extraordinary succulent upright leaves are about $1/2$ to $1^1/2$ inches, although they may grow a bit longer under less harsh conditions in cultivation. Their flower spikes emerge from developing growths and flaunt one to four flowers that face upward and are of narrow-segmented *Cattleya* form. Bright sunshine and ample water at the roots during the growing season are essential once the plants are established.

Neolehmannia porpax (*Epidendrum porpax*) is definitely whimsical. The species is a mat-forming creeper, and each stem bears a single flower, which at one inch is large for the size of the plant. Its dominant feature is the lip, which resembles a shiny red-maroon grape, and the narrow greenish dorsal sepal and petals frame it like a corona of exclamation points. This Central and South American species is easy to grow and prefers to be mounted so that it can ramble. Moderate light suits it well.

From southern Japan comes *Neofinetia falcata,* the Japanese wind orchid, a wonderful species for those who appreciate fragrance. Its cluster of showy, pure white flowers exudes a very strong sweet scent at night, sufficient to perfume a room. Vegetatively this orchid resembles a narrow-leafed *Ascocentrum miniatum,* but it does not require as much sun. The species has been hybridized with related genera to make a fine series of plants which, although a bit larger, are still dwarf and bear flowers of rose-pink, orange, coral, and lavender-blue—but some lack fragrance.

While *Oncidium onustum* has been known to grow epiphytically upon cacti in dry areas of Ecuador, harsh native growing conditions do not seem to have resulted in a demanding plant. Although it is small, with short, heavy leaves and fat pseudobulbs, both red-mottled, the gracefully arching flower spike can reach 20 inches. It bears many one-inch, flat, golden yellow flowers in a double rank, the lip making up 75 percent of the flower. It revels in very strong light, and when in active growth it requires frequent watering combined with rapid drainage such as it would receive on cork or tree fern mounts. Water should be reduced after flowering.

The West Indian equitant or fan oncidiums (now known as *Tolumnia*), such as *Oncidium pulchellum, O. variegatum, O. guianense,* and *O. triquetum,* are a group of

Leptotes bicolor 'Piping Rock' requires bright light and not much water at the roots.

jewellike species, with lavender, white and brown, yellow and brown, and red and beige flowers, respectively. Bloom spikes of varying length, depending on the species, issue from two- to four-inch fans of narrow, hard, channeled leaves and bear clusters of 3/4- to $1^{1}/_{2}$-inch blooms. The spikes often rebloom several times by producing accessory branches. Culturally, they require good light and excellent drainage on a mount or in a very small clay pot, combined with frequent watering. Hundreds of hybrids, many spectacularly colored and patterned, have been made within this group and require identical culture.

Similar in growth habit to the above but very different in flower is *Ornithocephalus bicornis*. The tiny, intricate white and green flowers are produced from a perfect fan of soft leaves, which may orient itself sideways or upside-down. The flower structure resembles a bird's head and beak, and the generic name means "bird head" or, to some "bird brain"! Shade and moisture suit this species, which is found in Mexico. Easy to grow *Pleurothallis grobyi* of the American tropics is a true miniature, its wand-like racemes of tiny chartreuse flowers rising well above the quarter-inch fleshy, orbicular leaves. Moderate light, frequent watering, and good drainage will maintain this species in good condition on a mount or in a pot.

Trichocentrum pfavii from Costa Rica produces its $1^{1}/_{4}$-inch brown, white, and rose flowers with frilly lips, several to the growth. The leaves are short and thick. It too can be grown in moderate light on a mount or in a pot.

Intermediate- to Cooler-Temperature Miniatures

Flowering best at the cooler end of the intermediate temperature range, *Dendrobium bellatulum* is a handsome miniature. Stumpy pseudobulbs are clothed with several silvery gray leaves, and from the top, one or two surprisingly large, showy flowers emerge, generally in the fall or winter. White sepals and petals frame a spectacular lip, which is deep orange at the base, becoming pale egg-yolk yellow near the end. The plant performs best with high light and needs a drier rest prior to flowering, corresponding with the end of the monsoon period in its native Thailand.

Dryadella lilliputana looks like a tiny green pincushion studded with quarter-inch flowers resembling tiny three-legged starfish, yellowish with dark dots. A slightly larger version is *Dryadella edwallii*. Both occur on scrubby trees in areas of Brazil and enjoy moderate light and a fair amount of water.

Oncidium cheirophorum is a lovely dwarf species that is a pleasure to grow. Chunky dark-speckled pseudobulbs and short, thin leaves are the backdrop for late-fall flowering of six-inch branched spikes holding myriads of highly fragrant small flowers, the mass resembling golden yellow popcorn. Growing on trees along middle-elevation streams in Costa Rica and Panama, this species requires bright light and frequent watering in small pots.

Almost insectlike is *Restrepia antennifera*. Paddle-shaped, pointed leaves on thin stems support a succession of relatively large flowers from the juncture of stem and leaf, the most showy portion being the lateral sepals, joined in a boat-shaped body with either a yellow or white background heavily spotted with maroon. The dorsal sepal and petals are reduced to threadlike structures equipped with enlarged clublike ends reminiscent of butterfly antennae. Shade, moisture, and moderately cool temperatures will emulate the conditions of the this plant's native Colombian Andes.

Restrepia antennifera 'Greentree': The dorsal sepals and petals of the species have clublike ends reminiscent of butterfly antennae.

For More Information

All About Orchids
Charles Marden Fitch
Doubleday, 1981

*A Culture Manual for Angraecoid Orchid Growers**
Fred Hillerman
American Orchid Society, 1992

*Encyclopaedia of Cultivated Orchids**
Alex D. Hawkes
Faber and Faber, London, 1987

Fundamentals of Orchid Biology
Joseph Arditti
John Wiley & Sons, 1992

Growing Orchids
Revised edition
James Watson, Editor
American Orchid Society, 2002

Growing Orchids Under Lights
Charles Marden Fitch
American Orchid Society, 2002

The Handbook on Orchid Nomenclature and Registration
Fourth Edition
International Orchid Commission, 1993

* *These books are out of print but worth hunting for secondhand.*

The Manual of Cultivated Orchid Species: Third Edition
Helmut Bechtel, Phillip Cribb, and Edmund Launert
MIT Press, 1992

Miniature Orchids and How to Grow Them
Rebecca Tyson Northen
Dover Publications, 1996

The Orchids: Natural History and Classification
Robert L. Dressler
Harvard University Press, 1990

The Orchids: Scientific Studies
Carl L. Withner, editor
Krieger Publishing, 1999

The Paphiopedilum Grower's Manual
Lance A. Birk
Pisang Press, 1983

Vandas and Ascocendas and Their Combinations with Other Genera
David L. Grove
Timber Press, 1995

Ultimate Orchid
Thomas J. Sheehan
DK Publishing, 2001

Anyone who loves plants won't want to miss the brand-new headquarters of the American Orchid Society, in Delray Beach, Florida.

The American Orchid Society

With almost 30,000 members around the globe, the American Orchid Society (AOS) is the largest organization in the world devoted exclusively to education, research, production, conservation, use, and appreciation of orchids. In 2001 its new headquarters in Delray Beach, Florida, opened to the public. For information about the AOS, visit its web site at www.aos.org.

The AOS is known for its publications: *Orchids*, a full-color monthly magazine about orchids and how to grow them, and *Awards Quarterly*, an indexed periodical that showcases award-winning orchids.

A brainchild of the AOS, the first World Orchid Conference was held in St. Louis in 1954. Since then, the event has been held every three years around the globe. For more information, contact the AOS, 16700 AOS Lane, Delray Beach, Florida 33446.

Nursery Sources

Cal-Orchid, Inc.
1251 Orchid Drive
Santa Barbara, CA 93111
805-967-1312
www.calorchid.com

Everglades Orchids
1101 Tabit Road
Belle Glade, FL 33430
561-996-9600
www.evergladesorchids.com

Fordyce Orchids
1330 Isabel Avenue
Livermore, CA 94550
925-447-1659
www.fordyceorchids.com

H & R Nurseries
841-240 Hihimanu Street
Waimanalo, Oahu, HI 96795
808-259-9626

Hoosier Orchid Company
8440 West 82nd Street
Indianapolis, IN 46278
888-291-6269
www.hoosierorchid.com

J & L Orchids
20 Sherwood Road
Easton, CT 06612
203-261-3772
www.jlorchids.com

Parkside Orchid Nursery
2503 Mountainview Drive
Ottsville, PA 18942
610-847-8039
www.parksideorchids.com

Piping Rock Orchids
2270 Cook Road
Galway, NY 12074
518-882-9002
www.pipingrockorchids.com

R.F. Orchids
28100 S.W. 182nd Avenue
Homestead, FL 33030
305-245-4570
www. rforchids.com

Santa Barbara Orchid Estate
1250 Orchid Drive
Santa Barbara, CA 93111
800-553-3387
www.sborchid.com

Contributors

Special thanks to the **American Orchid Society** for allowing Brooklyn Botanic Garden to adapt its culture sheets for *The Best Orchids for Indoors.*

Milton Carpenter, who consulted on the chapter about oncidiums, has been growing orchids for 40 years and is the owner of Everglades Orchids, Inc., in Belle Glade, Florida. He is a former president of the American Orchid Society and an accredited judge for the AOS, as well as past president of the Orchid Society of the Palm Beaches.

Phillip Cribb was educated at the Universities of Cambridge and Birmingham, England. He joined the staff of the Royal Botanic Gardens, Kew, in 1974 and is currently deputy keeper of the Herbarium and curator of the Orchid Herbarium. His current research is concentrated on the *Genera Orchidacearum* (*GO*) project, a new classification of the family, and on the taxonomy of tropical orchids. He is the author or co-author of some 30 books and over 350 papers on orchids.

Glen Decker has grown orchids for 26 years and received more than 100 American Orchid Society awards. He is presently the chairman of Publications for the AOS and the proprietor of Piping Rock Orchids, in upstate New York.

Wayne Ferrell is the manager of Santa Barbara Orchid Estate in Santa Barbara, California. He started working there in 1987 as an accountant and handyman but before long was helping with orchid cultivation. He enjoys all orchid genera, but cymbidiums are his favorite.

David L. Grove is an American Orchid Society judge and author of *Vandas and Ascocendas and Their Combinations with Other Genera,* published by Timber Press; he has also written numerous articles on the *Vanda* Alliance in orchid journals.

Carlos Fighetti has been growing orchids for almost three decades. He specializes in *Phalaenopsis* and paphiopedilums and has received more than 75 American Orchid Society awards. He is vice-president of the AOS and chair of its Historical and Library Committee as well as an accredited AOS judge. He has also served as president of the Greater New York Orchid Society and was the founding president of the International *Phalaenopsis* Alliance. He has written several articles for *Orchids* magazine and lectured at the World Orchid Congress.

Cordelia Head and Marguerite Webb, together with Lucinda Winn, own J & L Orchids, a company specializing in miniature orchids and unusual species. Cordelia is on several international conservation committees, and Marguerite has written many articles on masdevallias and related genera. Both have lectured extensively in the United States and abroad, including at World Orchid Conferences.

David Horak has been growing orchids for more than 25 years. He is the curator of orchids and the Robert W. Wilson Aquatic House at Brooklyn Botanic Garden. He is the current president of the Greater New York Orchid Society and the chairman of the New York International Orchid Show.

Charles Marden Fitch is an internationally known horticulturist and media specialist. He is the author of many books, including *All About Orchids, The Complete Book of Houseplants, Orchid Photography,* and *The Rodale Book of Garden Photography.* His photos have appeared in TV and video productions, magazines, newspapers, package designs, advertisements, and books such as *Ultimate Orchid, The World Wildlife Fund Book of Orchids,* and several encyclopedias.

Ned Nash has been an "orchid guy" all his professional life. He is a well-known and widely respected judge for the American Orchid Society, and most recently, he has been director of Education and Conservation for the AOS. He recently moved back to California to join Cal-Orchid, Inc.

H. Phillips Jesup has been growing orchids since 1952. He is active in several orchid societies and is a judge for the American Orchid Society.

Thomas W. Purviance and John F. Salventi began growing orchids as a hobby with 200 orchids in a bow window. Their "addiction" grew over the years and finally resulted in Parkside Orchid Nursery. Today, with five greenhouses, Parkside is one of the largest orchid nurseries in the northeastern United States.

Illustrations
Paul Harwood

Photos
Charles Marden Fitch all photos, except where noted
Glen Decker page 13 left
Rod Peakall pages 14 both, 16 both, 17
Bonnie Sangster pages 48, 51 right

Index

Orchids that have arrived by mail, ready to grow.

More Information on Growing Orchids

The companion to *The Best Orchids for Indoors, The Gardener's Guide to Growing Orchids* includes step-by-step instructions on potting and repotting, watering, fertilizing, propagation, and more.

Brooklyn Botanic Garden

World renowned for pioneering gardening information, Brooklyn Botanic Garden's award-winning guides provide practical advice for gardeners in every region of North America.

Join Brooklyn Botanic Garden as an annual Subscriber Member and receive three gardening handbooks, delivered directly to you, each year. Other benefits include free admission to many public gardens across the country, plus three issues of *Plants & Gardens News, Members News,* and our guide to courses and public programs.

For additional information on Brooklyn Botanic Garden, including other membership packages, call 718-623-7210 or visit our web site at www.bbg.org. To order other fine titles published by BBG, call 718-623-7286 or shop in our online store at www.bbg.org/gardengiftshop.